WEAPONS OF WAR

WARSHIPS
INSIDE & OUT

ROBERT JACKSON

ROSEN
PUBLISHING®

New York

This edition first published in 2012 by:

The Rosen Publishing Group, Inc.
29 East 21st Street
New York, NY 10010

Project Editor: Sarah Uttridge
Picture Research: Terry Forshaw
Design: Nicola Hibberd

Library of Congress Cataloging-in-Publication Data

Warships: inside & out/Robert Jackson.
     p. cm.—(Weapons of war)
Includes bibliographical references and index.
ISBN 978-1-4488-5981-8 (library binding)
1. Warships—History—Juvenile literature. I. Title.
V765.J33 2012
623.82509—dc23

2011030658

Manufactured in the United States of America

CPSIA Compliance Information: Batch #W12YA: For further information, contact Rosen Publishing, New York, New York, at 1-800-237-9932.

Photo Credits: Art-Tech/Aerospace: 5, 55, 60, 85; Art-Tech/MARS: 6, 79, 113; BAE Systems: 155; Cody Images: 4, 7, 30, 37, 42, 43, 48, 49, , 54, 61, 66, 67, 72, 73, 78, 84, 90, 91, 100, 180, 112, 131, 154; Kockums: 95, 148, 149; Library of Congress: 24; Mary Evans Picture Library: 36 (Suddeutsche Zeitung); Photo 12: 19; Photos.com: 18; TopFoto: 25 (Granger Collection); U.S. Department of Defense: 31, 92, 93, 94, 101, 106, 107, 118, 119, 124, 125, 130, 142, 143; Wikipedia Creative Commons Licence: 12 (Musee Marine); All artworks courtesy of Art-Tech/Aerospace and De Agostini except for the following: BAE Systems: 140–141; John Batchelor: 138–139; Kockums: 144–145; Military Visualisations Inc: 122–123, 146–147, 152–153; Navy News: 150–151; Tony Gibbons courtesy of Bernard Thornton Artists, London: 10–11, 22–23, 28–29

Contents

Classic Ships 1859–1949   4

Modern Ships 1950–Present   92

Classic Ships 1859–1949

In 1860, the appearance of a new French warship caused great consternation in Britain. She was *Gloire*, and she was the first armored warship in the world. Her deployment set off an arms race that was to last for decades.

Shikishima *was still afloat at Sasebo at the end of World War II, having somehow managed to escape American air attacks, but she had not moved under her own power for two decades. She was broken up in 1948.*

The *Gloire*, and all the other warships that appear in this fascinating book, had one thing in common: they were built to fight, either on the surface of the sea or beneath it. In these pages, the reader will find a step-by-step guide to the development of warships over the past

century and a half. The pages on each individual vessel feature details of its internal workings as well as an in-depth account of its career.

In the last two decades of the nineteenth century, supremacy on the high seas unquestionably rested with Great Britain. New ideas and inventions were emerging so quickly that a new vessel could be obsolete before it was launched. In the 1890s the Royal Navy, closely followed by other major naval powers, developed a new standard type of battleship later known as the "pre-dreadnought." In all, forty-two pre-dreadnoughts were built for the Royal Navy up to 1904, and they laid down a firm pattern of capital ship construction that was quickly adopted by other seafaring nations.

MODERN NAVAL WARFARE

The era of modern naval warfare, however, began on May 27, 1905, on the other side of the world, when warships of the Russian Baltic Fleet – a force designated the 2nd Pacific Squadron – under Vice-Admiral Rozhdestvensky entered the Straits of Tsushima, at the entrance to the Sea of Japan,

having completed an incredible seven-month voyage from its home base. The voyage was in the nature of a punitive expedition, mounted in response to a damaging Japanese attack on the Russian naval base at Port Arthur in the previous year. The Battle of Tsushima, in which the Japanese destroyed the Russian naval force, showed the world what modern warships, crewed by well-trained men, could achieve against obsolete vessels with conscript crews.

It was in 1905, too, that the shape of naval warfare was changed forever with the launch of a single British battleship. She was HMS *Dreadnought*, a vessel that made all other warships obsolete overnight. This was a time of innovation, a period that saw the debut of the battlecruiser, a hybrid warship that was to make

If a proposal to upgrade the main armament to six 15-in (380-mm) guns in three twin turrets had been implemented, Scharnhorst *might have been a very formidable opponent, faster than any British capital ship.*

its mark on the sea battles of the twentieth century.

BRITAIN'S SUPREMACY CHALLENGED

The years that led up to World War I witnessed Great Britain's naval supremacy challenged first by Germany and then Japan, but at the end of that conflict the German High Seas Fleet had ceased to exist and the principal maritime powers were Britain, Japan and the United States, with France and Italy also in the running. Russia's naval strength, shattered by the Japanese fleet at Tsushima in 1905, had never recovered from that humiliation, and its post-war reconstruction was delayed by the economic effects of the Russian Revolution.

The years between 1905 and 1935 were marked by undreamed-of technological innovation. Destroyers, once little more than coastal craft, were turned into hardy, seaworthy vessels with a role to play on the world's oceans, and World War I proved the destructive capability of the submarine beyond all doubt. During that war, Britain took the first tentative steps in the development of the aircraft carrier, the vessel that was to become the capital ship of the future. The carrier, perhaps, was the most significant naval design to emerge in the 1905–35 period; not only did it enable fleets to engage one another at distances far beyond visual range, but it also became a primary tool in hunting down the two greatest naval threats of World War II, the commerce raider and the submarine.

Above, the battleship Bismarck *is pictured at completion. Center foregound, with his back to the camera, is Adolf Hitler, on a visit to the vessel. He was fascinated by battleships.*

Due to the cost-cutting policy that influenced her design, De Ruyter *was not quite up to task. Her main battery (5.9-in [7 x 150-mm] guns) was inadequate, despite having an excellent fire control system.*

Despite this, throughout the period of the 1920s and 1930s many traditionalists still remained convinced that any future naval battles would be decided by battleships, and at the beginning of World War II such vessels still represented the most powerful war machines made by man.

MOVING WITH THE TIMES

The attacks by torpedo aircraft on Taranto in 1940 and Pearl Harbor in 1941 changed the picture completely, proving that a battleship could not exist without control of the air space above it. The Pacific battles of 1942–45 saw the last major surface actions fought by battleships, and proved conclusively that the aircraft carrier was at the core of modern naval warfare. That picture, too, would alter over the next two decades, with the advent of the nuclear submarine.

"The moral effect of an omnipresent fleet is very great, but it cannot be weighed against a main fleet known to be ready to strike and able to strike hard."

Lord Fisher, First Sea Lord

Gloire 1859

France's *Gloire* was the first armored ship-of-the-line in the world, and the mother of all armored warships that came after her. She caused great consternation in British naval circles, her appearance setting off a naval arms race that was to last for decades.

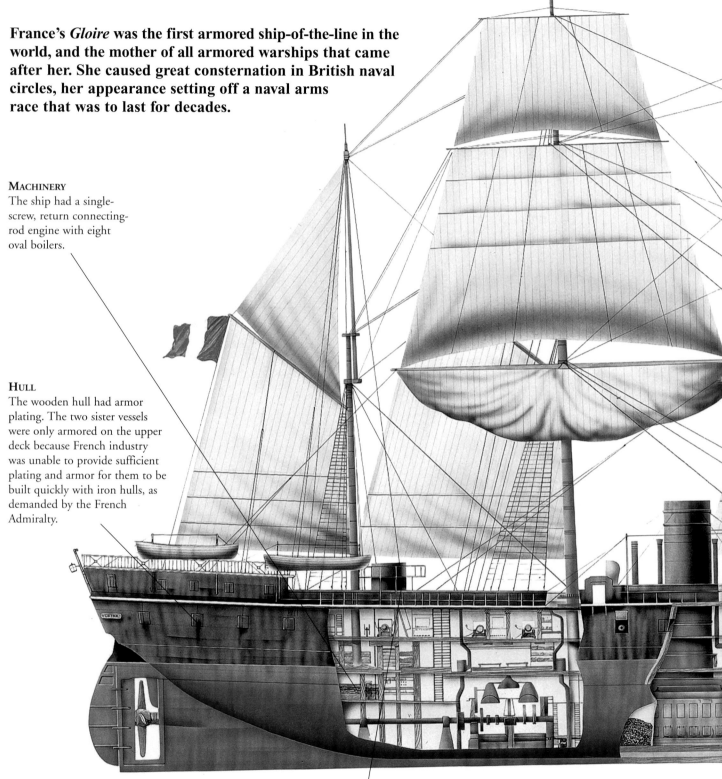

MACHINERY
The ship had a single-screw, return connecting-rod engine with eight oval boilers.

HULL
The wooden hull had armor plating. The two sister vessels were only armored on the upper deck because French industry was unable to provide sufficient plating and armor for them to be built quickly with iron hulls, as demanded by the French Admiralty.

ARMAMENT
The ship was originally fitted with 36 muzzle-loading guns of 6.4-in (163-mm) caliber, but these proved to have very poor hitting power against armor. They were later replaced by more powerful breechloaders.

ARMOR

The armored belt extended from stem to stern and from below the waterline to the upper deck, being backed by the wooden hull. The conning tower was unroofed, and there was an iron layer under the wooden upper deck.

RIG

Gloire was originally equipped with a light barquentine rig of 11,800 sq ft (1096 sq m), but to save on engine operating costs in peacetime this was changed to a full rig of 27,000 sq ft (2,508 sq m), much reduced at a later date.

F A C T S

- Launched November 24, 1859, completed July 1860.

- Two sister ships, *Invincible* and *Normandie*.

- Refitted and rearmed 1869.

- Discarded 1879, broken up 1883.

GLOIRE – SPECIFICATION

Country of origin: France
Type: Armored frigate
Laid down: April 1858
Builder: Toulon, France
Launched: November 24, 1859
Commissioned: August 1860
Decommissioned: 1879
Fate: Scrapped in 1883

Crew: 570 men

Dimensions:
Displacement: 6,206 tons (5,630 tonnes)
Length: 255 ft (77.8 m)
Beam: 55.8 ft (17 m)
Draught: 27.6 ft (8.4 m)

Power plant:
Propulsion:
    Sail: 11,800 sq ft (1,096 sq m)
    Machinery: Single-shaft HRCR (horizontal return) steam engine producing 2,500 hp (1.9 mW)
    Boilers: 8 oval boilers
Speed: 13 knots
Endurance: 733 tons (665 tonnes) of coal

Armament & Armor:
Armament: 1858–60 model:
    36 x 6.4-in (163-mm) rifled muzzle-loaders
    after 1866: 8 x 9-in (239-mm) BL model 1864; 6 x 7.6-in (193-mm) BL model 1866
Armor: 4.3–4.7-in (110–119-mm) iron plates

CREW

Gloire and her sister ships had a complement of 570, existing in cramped and uncomfortable conditions. In July 1862, *Normandie* became the first amored ship to cross the Atlantic to Mexico, but returned in the following year after a serious outbreak of yellow fever.

Gloire did not enjoy her prestige for long. Apart from the fact that she was soon overtaken by more modern designs, which relied on steam power alone, the rapid deterioration of her wooden hull components meant that she had an active life of less than 20 years before she was stricken.

GLOIRE

The French were lucky to have the leading naval architect of the day, Dupuy de Lôme. He took the design of his outstanding two-decker *Napoleon*, built in 1850, and modified it to carry iron side-plating strong enough to withstand the impact of the latest explosive shells fired by the 55-lb (25-kg) muzzle-loading gun. The result was *Gloire*, the world's first armored seagoing battleship. She was hardly a beautiful vessel, and she handled badly, but she temporarily gave the French a leading edge in warship technology.

Gloire was a direct result of French Emperor Napoleon III's ambition to establish a French empire in Mexico, which would require considerable naval forces to maintain.

The British victory at Trafalgar in 1805 effectively meant the end of France as a major naval power for half a century. In the middle of the nineteenth century, however, the French Emperor Napoleon III laid plans to return France to her former glory by expanding her empire overseas. In 1848, the French launched *Napoleon*, the first battleship designed to be powered by steam. A few years later, the Crimean War reinforced a growing understanding that, when it came to evading counterfire from shore batteries, ships with engines were far more useful and maneuverable than those with only the power of sail.

Close-up

Gloire's design was based on that of the steam frigate *Napoleon*, with a full-length battery along the hull. She was the first armored ship-of-the-line in the world and revolutionized naval warfare.

(1) **Masts:** *Gloire* retained masts and rigging. Her barquentine rig was later changed to full ship rig.

(2) **Lifeboats:** These were provided for the crew. Working conditions were hard on board because ventilation was poor and only oil lamps were available for lighting.

(3) **Single funnel:** *Gloire*'s single funnel was one of her distinguishing features. She was more or less identical to her sister ships, *Invincible* and *Normandie*.

(4) **Mainmast:** The ship was dominated by her huge mainmast. She had a short, tubby hull and was squat and ugly in appearance.

(5) **Rigging:** The admirals of *Gloire*'s day refused to countenance warships without rigging, but within a few short years even they realized rigging was an unnecessary encumbrance.

(6) **Hull:** French industry could not provide sufficient material for iron hulls quickly enough, so the hull was wooden, with only the deck featuring armor plating.

The French Fleet in harbor, with Gloire *at center. She is fitted with a bark rig in this picture. The ship on the right is* La Couronne, *which was a near sister ship, but with two gun decks.*

Naval firepower had also undergone a revolution in the first half of the nineteenth century. It began in 1822, when a French artilleryman named Henri Paixhans published a treatise on how the French Navy, shattered in its long war with Britain, could achieve parity with the Royal Navy without embarking on a massive and costly shipbuilding program. His solution was to adapt the hollow cast-iron mortar bomb, which had been in use for many years, to be fired by naval guns. If such a shell penetrated a ship's timbers, it would explode with enormous force and start uncontrollable fires, leading to a huge blast. The tremendous explosion that had destroyed Admiral Brueys' flagship *L'Orient* at the Battle of the Nile in August 1798 was deeply embedded in French naval memory.

BRITISH IDEAS

The British had similar ideas. Both navies began using the explosive shell at about the same time, the French issuing their new shell in 1824 for use with their 55-lb (25-kg) guns, and the British issuing their own shell for use with the tried-and-tested 68-lb (31-kg) gun some two years later. Both navies continued to use solid shot, however, because the cannons that fired it were more accurate over long ranges.

By the 1840s most three-deckers carried a combination of 60 percent solid shot cannon and 40 percent shell guns. Shells were fitted with a wooden fuse, which was ignited by the flash of a black powder charge as the gun was fired. A simple time delay prevented detonation until the projectile struck its target.

THE FIRST OF HER KIND

The French took the next step when they built *Gloire*, a vessel capable of withstanding such missiles. She had some radical features, including a blunt bow with a convex stem, and she was not without her faults. She had a low freeboard, which made it difficult for her main deck gunners to achieve the desired accuracy in a seaway, and the gunports were too close to the waterline and to each other, making working conditions crowded and difficult for the gunners. She was also disadvantaged by being rushed into service – her timbers had not been allowed to season over the usual three-year period.

Nevertheless, she was the first of her kind, and she paved the way for more successful vessels. The fourth in her class, the somewhat larger *Couronne*, had an iron hull. Launched in 1861, she was not discarded until 1910, and she was still afloat in 1934, when she was broken up.

Virginia 1861

The *Virginia* began life as the Union screw frigate *Merrimack*, which was raised and reconstructed by the Confederates after she had been burned at Norfolk to prevent capture. She was rebuilt as a casemate ironclad.

RAM
Concerned by reports that the Union Navy was planning to build an ironclad warship, and worried that *Virginia*'s guns would not have sufficient penetrating power to take on such a vessel, *Virginia*'s designers fitted her with a ram.

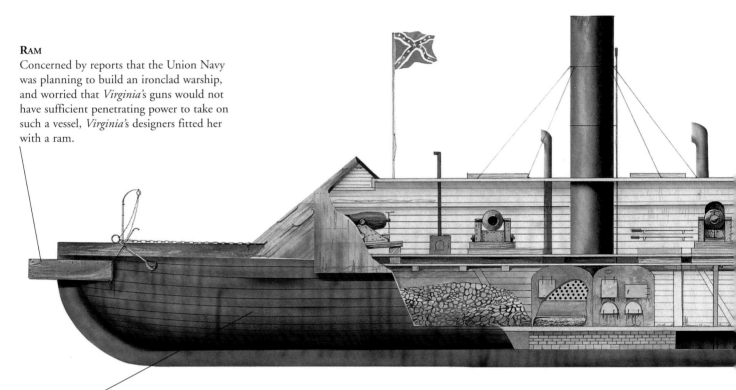

HULL
During reconstruction, the burnt hull timbers were cut down to the waterline, and a new deck and armored casemate were added. The *Virginia* set the pattern for all Confederate armored ships, with the forward and after parts of the hull awash except for a low coaming at the bows.

VIRGINIA – SPECIFICATION

Country of origin: Confederate States of America
Type: Ironclad ram
Laid down: 1862 (overlay USS *Merrimack*)
Launched: March 8, 1862
Commissioned: 1862
Decommissioned: n/a
Fate: Scuttled by crew, May 11, 1862
Complement: 320 officers and men

Dimensions:
Displacement: 4,500 tons (4,082 tonnes)
Length: 275 ft (84 m); **Beam:** 38.6 ft (11.8 m);
    Draught: 22 ft (6.7 m)

Power plant:
Propulsion: steam
Speed: 9 knots

Armament & Armor:
Armament: 2 x 12-lb (5-kg) howitzers; 2 x 7-in (178-mm) rifles; 2 x 6-in (152-mm) rifles; 6 x 9-in (229-mm) smoothbores
Armor: Double iron plating, 2-in (51-mm) thick

ARMAMENT

The battery consisted of four single-banded Brooke rifles and six 9-in (229-mm) Dahlgren smoothbore shell guns. Two of the rifles, bow and stern pivots, were 7-in (178-mm) weapons; the other two were 6-in (152-mm) rifles, one on each broadside.

FACTS

- Launched as the U.S. screw frigate *Merrimack* at Boston, June 14, 1855.

- Burnt to prevent capture at Norfolk in 1861.

- Refloated by Confederate Navy and rebuilt as ironclad named *Virginia*; completed in February 1862.

- Engaged *Monitor* at Battle of Hampton Roads, March 9, 1862; first engagement between ironclad warships.

- Run ashore and burnt by crew to prevent capture, James River, May 11, 1862.

MACHINERY

The Confederates discovered that *Merrimack's* single-shaft returning rod connecting engine was still intact and no plans were made to fit a new power plant. However, *Merrimack's* engine had not been very efficient to begin with, and struggled to cope with the *Virginia*, made much heavier by the addition of tons of armor and ballast.

ARMOR

The deck was protected by iron plate 4-in (102-mm) thick. The casemate was a laminate of oak and pine, topped with two 2-in (51-mm) layers of iron plating laid perpendicular to each other, and angled to deflect shot hits.

The success of the *Merrimack/Virginia*, or at least the promise of it, blinded the Confederates to any type of warship other than the casemate ironclad, and many vessels of this type were placed under construction.

MERRIMACK

MERRIMACK

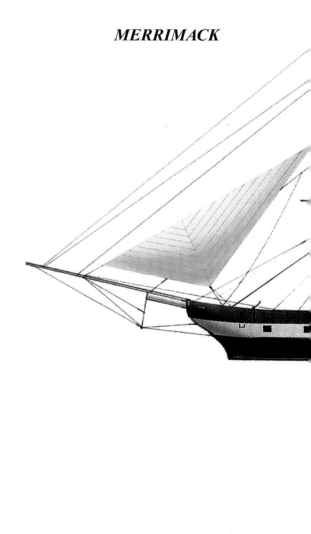

RIVAL: *MONITOR*

MERRIMACK

The rebuilding of the *Merrimack* gave the Confederate Navy a new type of fighting ship that promised to cancel out the Union's great superiority in conventional warships. Commissioned as *Virginia* in mid-February 1862, the ship's iron armor made her virtually invulnerable to contemporary gunfire. She carried 10 guns of her own, a 7-in (178-mm) pivot-mounted rifle at each end and a broadside battery of two 6-in (152-mm) rifles, and six 9-in (229-mm) smoothbores. Affixed to her bow was an iron ram, allowing the ship herself to be employed as a deadly weapon.

All the Confederate Navy's casemate ironclads were built in the southern ports, where they remained isolated. They were slow and non-seagoing. Many were never completed, while others lacked armor or were built with inefficient engines.

Virginia made her first combat sortie on March 8, 1862, steaming down the Elizabeth River from Norfolk and into Hampton Roads. Accompanied by other warships, her mission was to break the blockade imposed by the Union Navy, which had deployed the large sloop-of-war *Cumberland* and the smaller *Congress*. In an historic action that dramatically demonstrated the superiority of armored steam-powered warships over their wooden sailing counterparts, she rammed and sank the *Cumberland*, which broke off the *Virginia's* ram as she went down. The captain of the *Congress* ordered his ship to be beached in shallow water

Close-up

The Battle of Hampton Roads took place at a roadstead in Virginia where the Elizabeth and Nansemond rivers meet the James River just before it flows into Chesapeake Bay.

(1) **Flag:** The Confederate flag flies proudly from the *Virginia* at the Battle of Hampton Roads.

(2) **Virginia:** In action at Hampton Roads, which was arguably the most important naval engagement of the American Civil War in terms of future warship development.

(3) **Battle:** Amid the smoke of battle, *Monitor* and *Virginia* fought an inconclusive battle that lasted for approximately three hours.

(4) **Beached:** *Virginia* badly damaged the Union warship *Congress*, which was beached at the command of her captain.

(5) **Damage:** Shot from the grounded *Congress* and other warships riddled the *Virginia's* smokestack with holes and caused damage in other areas.

(6) **Turret:** *Monitor's* turret was steam trained, which meant that control was not highly precise.

In the aftermath of the Battle of Hampton Roads, the names Virginia *and* Merrimack *were used equally by both sides, as attested by the newspapers and correspondence of the day. This caused much confusion among later historians.*

and traded gunfire with *Virginia*, being eventually shelled into submission. In Washington, D.C., many of the Union government's senior officials panicked, convinced that *Virginia* posed a grave threat to Union seapower and coastal cities. They were unaware that her serious operational limitations, caused by her deep draught, weak power plant, and extremely poor seakeeping, essentially restricted her use to deep channels in calm, inland waterways.

Virginia did not emerge from the battle unscathed. As she was being shot at from *Cumberland* and *Congress*, shore-based Union troops riddled her smokestack. All of this combined to reduce her already low speed. Two of her guns were out of order, and a number of armor plates had been loosened. Nevertheless, she returned to Hampton Roads the next day to attack the grounded steam frigate *Minnesota*, which had run aground on a sandbank while trying to get away during the earlier action.

THREE-HOUR BATTLE

During the night, however, the ironclad Union ship *Monitor* had arrived and had taken a position to defend *Minnesota*. When *Virginia* approached, *Monitor* intercepted her. The two ironclads confronted each other in combat for about three hours, with neither able to inflict significant damage

on the other. The duel ended indecisively, *Virginia* returning to her home at the Gosport Navy Yard for repairs and strengthening, and *Monitor* turning back to her station defending *Minnesota*.

Over the next two months, the two ironclads kept each other in check. *Virginia*, having been repaired and strengthened at the Norfolk Navy Yard, re-entered the Hampton Roads area on April 11 and May 8, but no further combat with the *Monitor* resulted. As the Confederates abandoned their positions in the Norfolk area, *Virginia* was threatened with the loss of her base. After a futile effort to lighten the ship enough to allow her to move up the James River, on May 11 the *Virginia* was destroyed by her crew off Craney Island, some 6 miles (10 km) from where she had fought her engagements of March 8 and 9. *Virginia*'s wreck was largely removed between 1866 and 1876.

A TURNING POINT

There is no doubt this engagement – the first between two ironclad warships – inspired the world's navies to abandon the traditional pattern of wooden warship construction and concentrate instead on ironclad vessels. The *Virginia*'s success in sinking the *Cumberland* with her ram also persuaded navies to retain this feature as a viable weapon.

Maine 1890

Legislation authorizing the foundation of a new U.S. Navy was only passed in 1883, and progress was slow. The first two American battleships, the *Texas* and *Maine* of 1888, were little more than armored cruisers. Both were based on foreign designs.

MACHINERY
Power was provided by two Quintard vertical triple-expansion engines, with eight cylindrical boilers. These gave her a maximum speed of 17 knots.

BUNKERS
The coal bunkers were placed around the perimeter of the hull in the belief that this would afford extra protection, the magazines being positioned inboard of the bunkers.

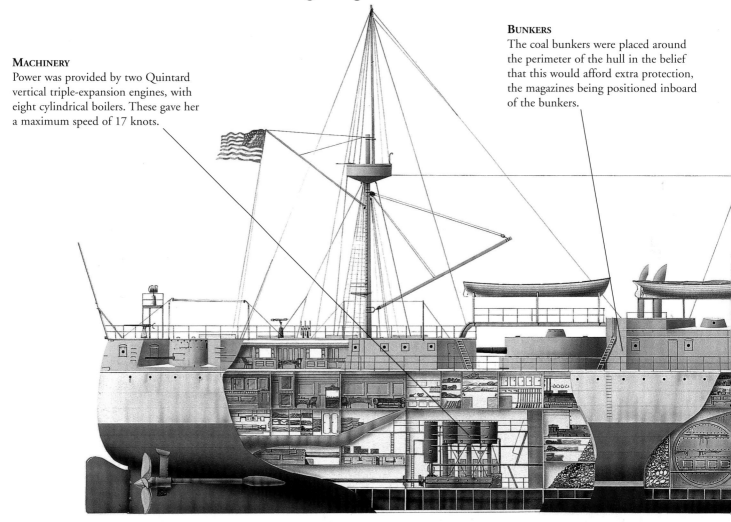

MAINE – SPECIFICATION

Country of origin: USA
Type: Pre-dreadnought battleship
Laid down: October 17, 1888
Builder: New York Naval Yard, Brooklyn, New York
Launched: November 18, 1890
Commissioned: September 17, 1895
Status: Remains scuttled in the Strait of Florida, March 16, 1912
Complement: 374 officers and men

Dimensions:
Displacement: 6,789 tons (6,159 tonnes)
Length: 324 ft 4 in (98.86 m)
Beam: 57 ft (17 m)

Draught: 22 ft 6 in (6.86 m)

Power plant:
Installed power: 9,293 hp (6,930 kW)
Propulsion: 2 shafts, 2 x vertical triple-expansion steam engines, 8 boilers
Speed: 17 knots
Range: 3600 nm (6670 km) at 10 knots

Armament & Armor:
Armament: 4 x 10-in (254-mm) guns; 6 x 6-in (152-mm) guns
Armor: 2–12 in (51–305 mm)

ARMAMENT
Maine and *Texas* were unusual in that their main armament was mounted *en echelon*, which meant it projected off to either side, severely limiting the ships' ability to fire a broadside.

ARMOR
Maine's armor belt was 180 ft (55 m) long and 6–11 in (152–279 mm) thick. The turrets were protected by 8 in (203 mm) and the barbettes by 12 in (305 mm). The deck carried 2–4 in (51–102 mm) of armor plating.

FACTS

- Launched November 18, 1890; completed 1895.

- North Atlantic, 1895–98.

- Destroyed by gas explosion in Havana harbor, 260 dead, 1898.

- Hulk refloated and sunk at sea, February 1912.

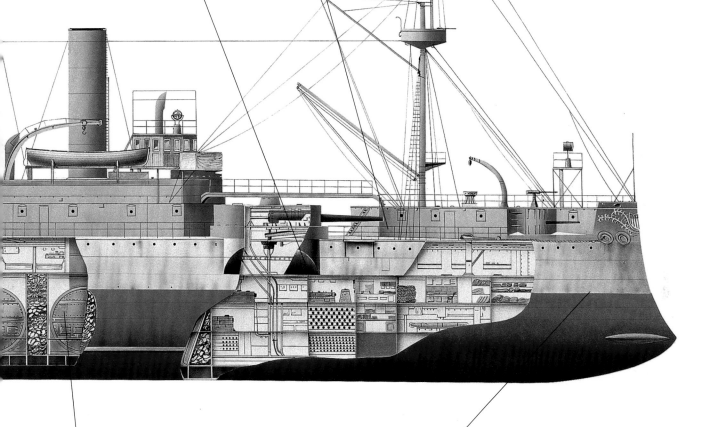

ENDURANCE
Maine's coal capacity was 895 tons (812 tonnes), which meant that she could not spend lengthy periods at sea. It also meant that she could not operate at high speed for any length of time, as coal consumption increased dramatically in these circumstances.

HULL
When *Maine* was completed and fully fitted out, it was found that the bow section had a draft 3 ft (1 m) deeper than the stern. This was caused not by a fault in the design, but a mistake in the loading plan. As a result, 8 tons (443.5 tonnes) of ballast had to be loaded near the stern, resulting in unplanned extra weight.

There have been four major investigations into the sinking of the *Maine* since 1898. Even today, experts cannot agree whether the explosion was caused by a mine or by spontaneous combustion in a coal bunker.

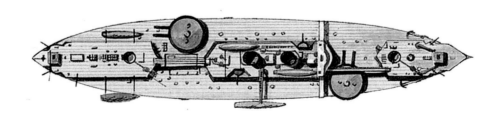

MAINE

The *Maine* arrived at Havana on January 25, 1898. The Spanish authorities in Havana were wary of American intentions, but they afforded Captain Charles Sigsbee and the officers of *Maine* every courtesy. In order to avoid the possibility of trouble, *Maine's* commanding officer did not allow his enlisted men to go on shore. Sigsbee and the consul at Havana, Fitzhugh Lee, reported that the navy's presence appeared to have a calming effect on the situation, and both recommended that the navy department send another battleship to Havana when it came time to relieve the *Maine*. Events were to take a very different turn.

Maine was the U.S. Navy's first battleship. Following her destruction, a second Maine, designated BB-10, was laid down in 1899, and served until 1920. A third Maine was ordered in 1940, but was cancelled.

The *Maine* and the *Texas* were the U.S. Navy's first true battleships. However, they were second-class vessels that would not have been a match for any capital ships built by any other major maritime power during this period.

In the United States, support for the building of new, modern warships was rather feeble in the latter half of the nineteenth century. Despite the success of the Union's ironclad warships in the Civil War, after the conflict ended interest in the navy waned, and monitors for coastal defense were thought to be the only necessary warships. No money was made available for building new ships, and new vessels, including five monitors, were surreptitiously built using funds provided for repairing old ones. It was not until 1883 that legislation was

passed for the building of a "New Navy," its first vessels to be based on foreign designs. What may be described as the "monitor mentality" was still strong, however, and the first of the new vessels, the *Indiana* class, were completed as coastal defense battleships with low freeboard.

MAINE'S CAREER

The *Maine* spent her active career operating along the East Coast of the United States and the Caribbean. In January 1898, she deployed from Key West, Florida, to Havana, Cuba, to protect U.S. interests during a local insurrection and civil disturbances. Three weeks later, on February 15 at 2140, an explosion on board the warship occurred in the Havana harbor. Later investigations revealed that more than 5.1 tons (5 tonnes) of powder charges for the vessel's 6- and 10-in (152- and 254-mm) guns had detonated, virtually obliterating the forward third of the ship.

The remaining wreckage rapidly settled to the bottom of the harbor. Most of the crew of the *Maine* were sleeping or resting in the enlisted quarters in the forwards part of the ship when the explosion occurred. As a result of the explosion, or shortly thereafter, 236 men lost their lives, and eight more died later from injuries. Captain Charles Sigsbee and most of the officers survived because their quarters were in the aft portion of the ship. Altogether, there were only 89 survivors, 18 of whom were officers. On March 28, the U.S. Naval Court of Inquiry in Key West declared that a naval mine had been the cause of the explosion.

The destruction of the *Maine* was a major contributory factor in the outbreak of the Spanish-American War in April 1898. The belief that a mine had caused the disaster was seen as provocation to go to war. A subsequent investigation of the wreck in 1911, when bottom hull plates around the forward's reserve magazine were found to have been bent inwards and back, seemed to confirm the theory that a mine had been responsible, and it was not until decades later that this explanation was seriously challenged. Another theory was advanced in 1976, suggesting that the fatal explosion had been caused by the spontaneous explosion of coal dust.

Interior view

The captain's cabin on the *Maine* was spacious. Access to it was through a door leading from a kind of lobby.

1. **Personal possessions:** The captain's possessions were confined to a few books, manuals, and personal photographs.

2. **Furniture:** The cabin was made a little brighter by a chintz-covered table and an armchair or two. This was the captain's office when the ship was in harbor.

3. **Air:** Two or three scuttles – portholes – provided light and air. The captain was able to enjoy the benefit of these as his cabin was clear of the armor belt.

4. **Enamel:** The cabin had lots of white enamel. The deckhead above was of rough, white-painted cork to prevent sweating.

5. **Corticene:** The deck of the cabin was gleaming with shellacked corticene, a cork-like material that prevented slipping.

6. On active duty the captain would use his sea cabin, up on the bridge, if his presence there was necessary.

Dreadnought 1906

Dreadnought **was the first battleship to feature a main armament of a single caliber. Her appearance initiated a naval arms race that was to reach global proportions by the onset of World War I in 1914.**

MACHINERY

Dreadnought was the first capital ship to be powered by steam turbines instead of the old triple-expansion engines, making her the fastest battleship in the world at the time of her completion.

COMPARTMENTS

Another major innovation was the elimination of longitudinal passageways between compartments below the main deck level. Connected compartments had been found to be a cause of weakness.

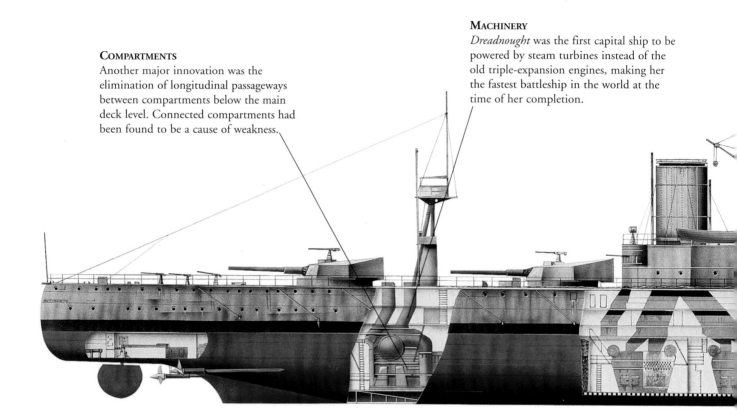

DREADNOUGHT – SPECIFICATION

Country of origin: United Kingdom
Type: Dreadnought
Laid down: October 2, 1905
Builder: HM Dockyard, Portsmouth
Launched: February 10, 1906
Commissioned: December 2, 1906
Decommissioned: 1919
Fate: Scrapped 1923
Complement: 695–773

Dimensions:
Displacement: 18,420 tons (16,710 tonnes)
Length: 527 ft (161 m)
Beam: 82 ft (25 m)
Draught: (26 ft (7.9 m)

Power plant:
Propulsion: 18 Babcock & Wilcox 3-drum water-tube boilers; Parsons direct drive steam turbines; 22,500 shp (17 MW) on four shafts
Speed: 21 knots
Range: 900/2,900 tons (816/2,630 tonnes) coal, 1,120 tons (1,016 tonnes) oil 6,620 nmi (12,260 km) at 10 knots 4,910 nmi (9,090 km) at 18.4 knots

Armor & Armament:
Armament: 10 x BL 12-in (305-mm) Mk X guns, 5 twin B Mk.VIII turrets (one forwards, two aft, two wing); 27 x 12-lb (5.4-kg) 18 cwt L/50 Mk.I guns, single mountings P Mk.IV; 5 x 18-in (457-mm) torpedo tubes (submerged);
Armor: 2.5–11 in (65–280 mm)

MAST

The tripod mast, which carried the fire control platform, was situated immediately behind the forward funnel so that the platform became very hot and filled with smoke when the ship was travelling at full speed, making it virtually useless. This and other design flaws were later corrected.

GUNNERY CONTROL

Instead of relying on voice pipes to transmit commands to the gun turrets, *Dreadnought* was fitted with electronic instruments for transmitting range and other data.

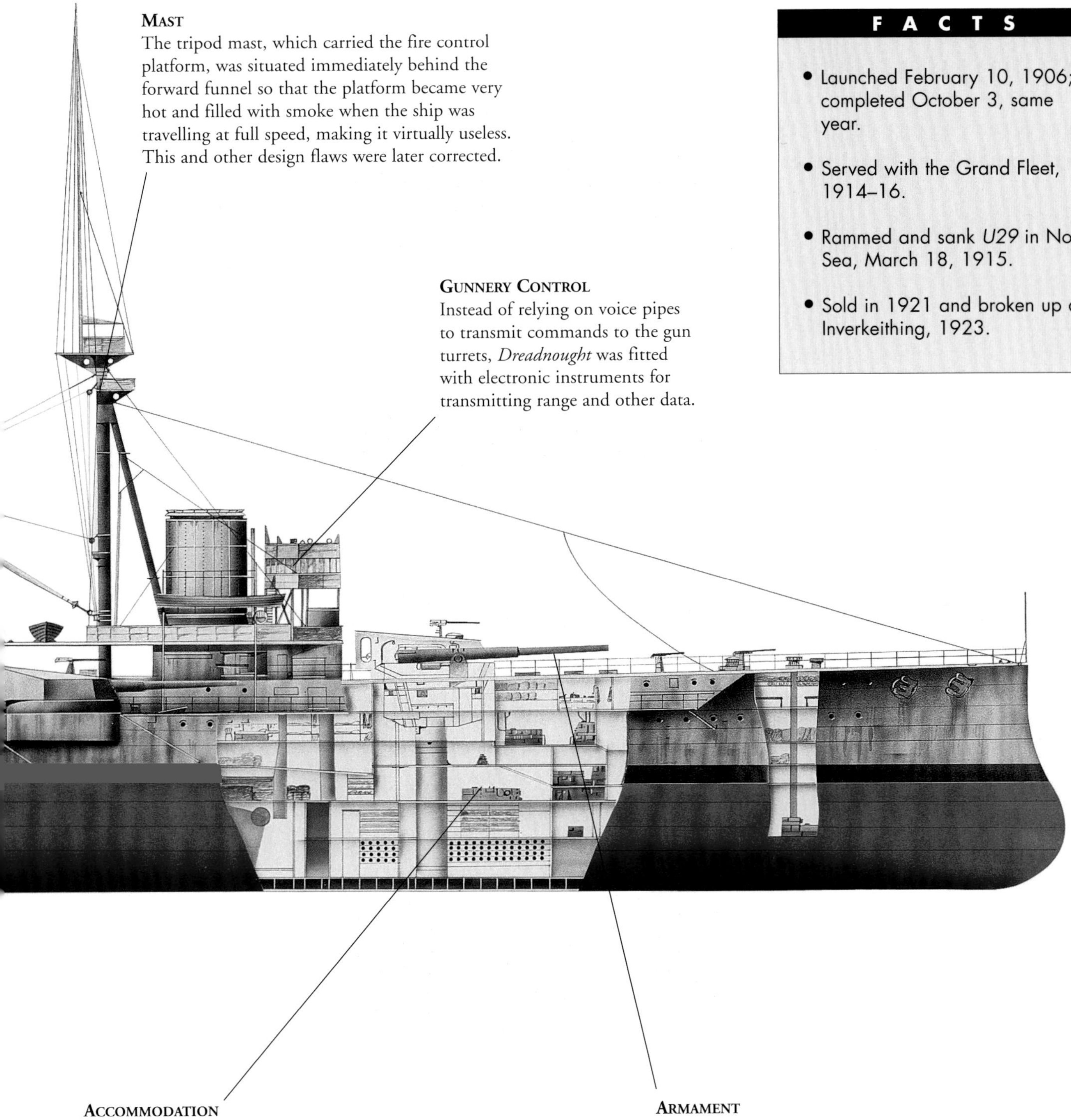

F A C T S

- Launched February 10, 1906; completed October 3, same year.

- Served with the Grand Fleet, 1914–16.

- Rammed and sank *U29* in North Sea, March 18, 1915.

- Sold in 1921 and broken up at Inverkeithing, 1923.

ACCOMMODATION

Sailing ships were controlled from the aft part of the ship, and officers were customarily housed aft. *Dreadnought* reversed the old arrangement, housing officers in the forward part of the ship and enlisted men aft so that both were closer to their action stations.

ARMAMENT

The use of guns of a uniform caliber made it much easier to adjust the fall of shot in action. All the shells had the same ballistic characteristics, so they would fall simultaneously in a cluster around the point of aim, whereas shells fired by mixed batteries had different flight times and tended to arrive sporadically.

Once the concept of the dreadnought had been proven, construction of this revolutionary type of battleship proceeded rapidly, at the rate of three or four a year. As a result, by 1913, 31 more were either in service or due to be commissioned.

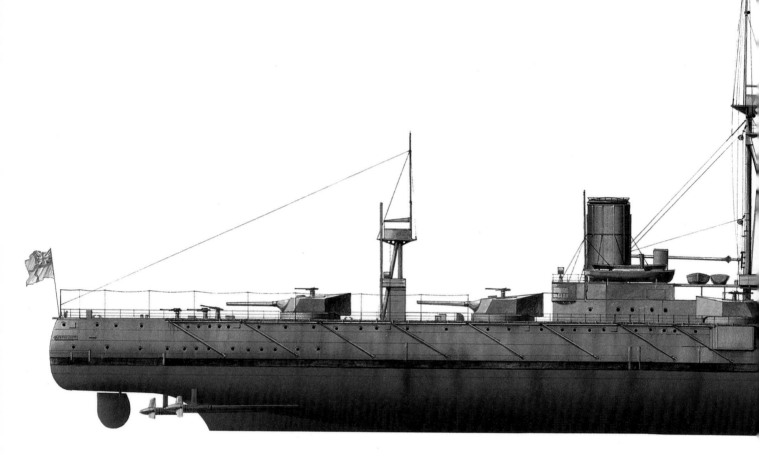

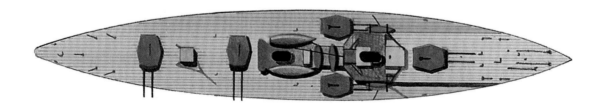

DREADNOUGHT

Critics claimed that the introduction of the dreadnoughts made the great mass of British battleships obsolete and vulnerable, but supporters of the concept had come to realize that secondary armament was now of minor importance. The increasing range of torpedoes was making close-in actions dangerous. Gunnery experts understood that at the immense ranges – 14,000 yards (12,810 m) or more – now possible for 12-in (305-mm) guns – only the biggest guns would count. Effective ranging depended on the firing of salvoes of shells and of a greater number in the salvo, and a full salvo from a dreadnought meant that 3.79 tons (3.85 tonnes) of high explosive was on its way to the enemy almost 18 nm (15 km) away.

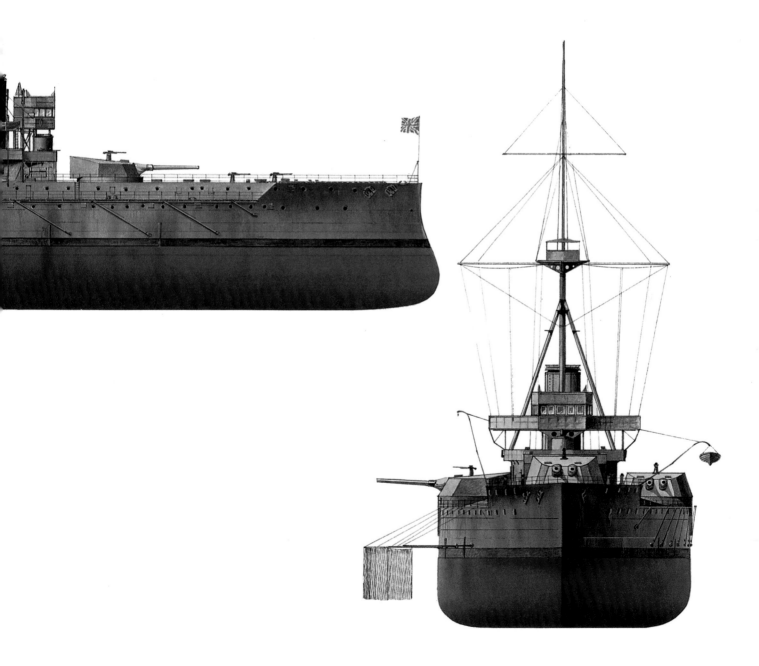

Dreadnought, *seen here in harbor, is readily distinguished by her massive tripod foremast. By 1916, however, she was considered too slow, and consequently did not see action in the Battle of Jutland.*

In the last two decades of the nineteenth century, supremacy on the high seas unquestionably rested with Great Britain. Unprecedented ideas and inventions were emerging so quickly that a new vessel could be rendered obsolete before it could even be launched.

Much of this problem was created by Britain's own naval policy, described as a "two-power standard," which kept the Royal Navy equal in numbers to any two foreign navies. In simple terms, warships were being built at too fast a rate to incorporate the latest technological advances.

In 1889, the two-power standard was modified somewhat when the Naval Defense Act came into force, decreeing that the Royal Navy must be capable of matching the world's second- and third-largest navies. The result was a new phase of shipbuilding, and at its forefront was the *Royal Sovereign* class of battleship. A highly successful design, they were faster than any contemporary battleships.

In the 1890s the Royal Navy, closely followed by other major naval powers, developed a new standard type of battleship later known as the "pre-dreadnought." The first was the 13,831-ton (12,548-tonne) *Renown* of 1892, but it was the *Majestic* class of 1893–94 that served as the pattern for battleship design for the next decade. Displacing 13,724 tons (15,129 tonnes), they were armed with four 12-in (305-mm) guns, 16 3-in (76-mm) guns and 1.85-in (1247-mm) guns, as well as five 18-in (457-mm) torpedo tubes. In all, 42 pre-dreadnoughts were built for the Royal Navy up to 1904.

BATTLESHIPS REVOLUTION

The true revolution in battleship design began with the appointment of Admiral Sir John Fisher as First Sea Lord in 1904. "Jackie" Fisher, as he was known throughout the service, was a comparative rarity in the Royal Navy of the day in that he was a senior officer with a firm grasp of scientific and technological principles. By the time he took over as First Sea Lord at the age of 58, Fisher had already put a lot of consideration into the concept of a battleship armed with a maximum number of 10-in (254-mm) guns at the expense of secondary armament. Within weeks of his appointment in 1904, Fisher convened a committee to design a battleship armed with the maximum number of 12-in (305-mm) guns, which was the caliber that the admiralty preferred. The committee was also meant to study a second type of warship, which would carry a battery of 12-in (305-mm) guns but which would have a speed of 24 knots or thereabouts. This vessel would be somewhat of a hybrid, in that it would be a cross between a heavy cruiser and a battleship. In other words, it was to be a battlecruiser.

"SUPER BATTLESHIP"

The concept of a "super battleship" took shape rapidly, its development spurred on by the acceleration of the international naval arms race, and a prototype was laid down by Portsmouth Dockyard in October 1905. It was constructed in great secrecy and in record time, the vessel being ready for initial sea trials a year and a day later. The name given to the formidable new ship was *Dreadnought*. In one stroke, she swept away all previous concepts of battleship design and launched naval strategy into an entirely new era.

Close-up

Dreadnought brought about a revolution in naval warship design, altering almost every aspect of the battleships of her day. She also initiated a naval arms race that would endure for decades.

(1) **Rear mast:** The rearmost of *Dreadnought's* two masts supported communications and other essential equipment.

(2) **Main turret:** *Dreadnought's* massive main turrets were protected by 11 in (279 mm) of armor plating. Her design rendered all other battleships obsolete overnight.

(3) **Armor:** *Dreadnought's* decks carried varying thicknesses of armor, ranging from 1–4 in (26–102 mm). Her armored bulkheads were 8 in (203 mm) thick.

(4) **Heavy guns:** From 1906 onwards a first-class battleship was defined as one capable of firing 10 heavy guns on either side.

(5) **Secondary armament:** This was now of reduced importance, the development of the torpedo having made close-in engagements too dangerous.

(6) **Turret guns:** *Dreadnought* was revolutionary in that she was armed with 10 12-in (305-mm) guns, two in each of five turrets placed on the centerline.

U9 1910

U9 was the lead boat of a class of four German submarines laid down in 1910, and the only one to survive World War I. She achieved some spectacular successes during her career under the command of Germany's first U-boat ace, Kapitänleutnant Otto Weddigen.

MACHINERY
U9 was powered by four Körting kerosene engines plus two electric motors. Range was 1,800 nm (3,334 km) at 14 knots on the surface, or 80 nm (148 km) at 5 knots submerged.

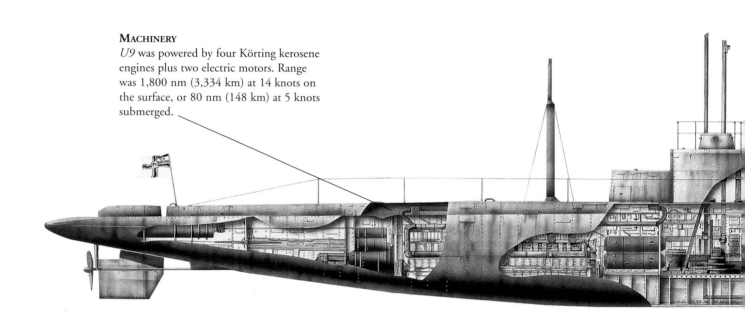

U9 – SPECIFICATION

Country of origin: Germany
Type: Submarine
Builder: Kaiserliche Werft, Danzig
Launched: February 22, 1910
Commissioned: April 18, 1910
Decommissioned: N/A
Fate: Surrendered November 26, 1918;
    Broken up at Morecambe, UK, in 1919
Complement: 29

Dimensions:
Displacement (surfaced): 425 tons (385.5 tonnes)
Displacement (submerged): 601 tons (545 tonnes)
Length: 188 ft (57.3 m)
Beam: 19.7 ft (6 m)
Draught: 11.5 ft (3.5 m)

Power plant:
Propulsion: Two-shaft kerosene engines/electric motors

Speed (surfaced): 14.2 knots
Speed (submerged): 8 knots
Range: 1,800 nm (3,334 km)

Armament:
4 x 18-in (457-mm) torpedo tubes (two bow, two stern; six
    torpedoes); 1 x 1.45-in (37-mm) deck gun

Service record
Part of: Kaiserliche Marine: I Flottille
Commanders:
    August 1, 1914–January 11, 1915: Otto Weddigen
    January 12, 1915–April 19, 1916: Johannes Spiess
Operations: 7
    August 1, 1914–July 7, 1915: I Flotilla
    July 7, 1915–April 19, 1916: Baltic Flotilla
    April 20, 1916–November 11, 1918: Training Flotilla
Victories: 14 ships sunk for a total of 9,715 tons (8,813 tonnes)
4 warships sunk for a total of 43,350 tons (39,326 tonnes)

TORPEDOES
The torpedo room was at the forward part of the cylindrical pressure hull. It contained two torpedo tubes and two reserve torpedoes. There were two further torpedo tubes in the stern.

BRIDGE
A small bridge was set on top of the conning tower, and a detachable rubber strip was mounted on stanchions along the deck to give crew protection when the boat was travelling on the surface.

FACTS

- Launched 1910 at Danzig.

- Sank the British cruisers *Hogue*, *Cressy*, and *Aboukir* off the Netherlands, September 22, 1914.

- Sank the British cruiser *Hawke* in the North Sea, October 15, 1914.

- Relegated to training duties, 1916.

- Surrendered 1918 and scrapped at Morecambe, UK, 1919.

CONNING TOWER
The conning tower was fitted with two periscopes, and also contained 24 levers for releasing air from the ballast tanks, electrical control gear for depth steering, a depth indicator, voice pipes, and the electrical torpedo-firing switches.

VENTILATION
The storage battery cells, which were located under the living spaces and filled with acid and distilled water, generated hydrogen gas on charge and discharge. This was drawn off through the ventilation system.

ACCOMMODATION
The officers' and warrant officers' accommodations were immediately aft of the torpedo room. These were separated from the main crew accommodations by a watertight bulkhead. Most of the crew slept in hammocks.

In 1914 Germany had not yet fully realized the potential of the submarine. However, as the war progressed, so did the importance of the submarine arm, until in 1916 and later years it was the main offensive arm of the German Navy.

DEADLY SUBMARINES

Germany's submarines struck the first blow in the conflict that was to come, and proved how deadly submarines could be to unprotected surface shipping. Strangely enough, the German naval staff at the turn of the century failed to appreciate the potential of the submarine, and the first submarines built in Germany were three "Karp" class vessels ordered by the Imperial Russian Navy in 1904. Germany's first practical submarine, *U1*, was not completed until 1906. She was, however, one of the most successful and reliable of the time.

REPLACEMENT: *DEUTSCHLAND*

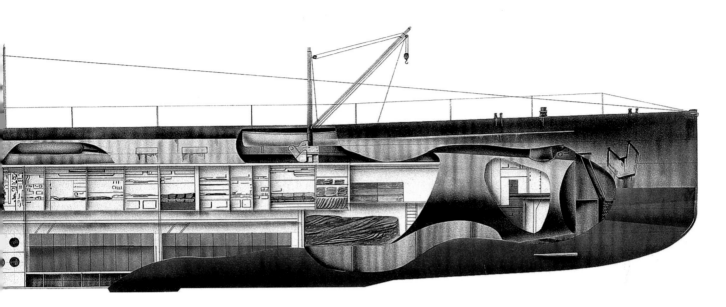

U9

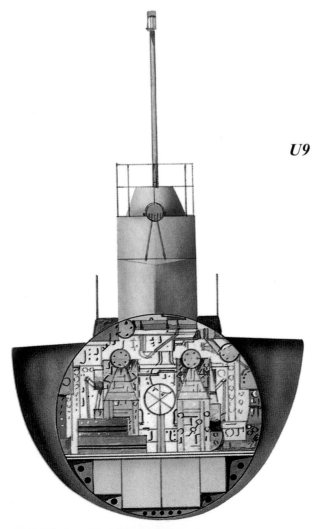

Although the Germans got to a slow start in their submarine construction program before World War I, from the start, the vessels were well engineered and used double hulls and twin screws. German engineers refused to install gasoline engines in the early boats, preferring to use smellier but safer kerosene fuel. Diesel engines were used later on.

The *U9* was one of the first U-boats to set out on a war patrol at the outbreak of World War I, and it was not long before success came her way. On September 22, 1914, she was patrolling south of the Dogger Bank when Otto Weddigen sighted three elderly cruisers of the British 7th Cruiser Squadron. They were the *Aboukir*, *Hogue*, and *Cressy*. A fourth cruiser had returned to port two days earlier for refuelling, while a force of destroyers, which should have been accompanying the cruisers, had become separated in heavy weather.

Close-up

In this German propaganda photograph, Captain Otto Weddigen and his officers are preparing to provide survivors of a sunken merchant ship with food and drink.

(1) **Conning tower:** This was the nerve center of the boat, as its name implies, and was very difficult to spot because of its small size.

(2) **Footholds:** Access to the U-boat's bridge could be gained from the deck by these footholds made in the side of the conning tower casing.

(3) **Boathook:** The German sailor is using a boathook to pull the merchant vessel's lifeboat alongside.

(4) **Supplies:** In general, Germany's U-boats were far better stocked with food and drink than their British counterparts.

(5) **Survivors:** Because there was no room for prisoners aboard a submarine, survivors were generally given food and drink, and then offered directions to the nearest land.

(6) **Surface warfare:** Most submarine actions in World War I were fought on the surface with gunfire.

The U9 *returns home after a successful war patrol. With the United States already on the side of the Allies, Germany announced on January 31, 1917, that its U-boats would engage in unrestricted submarine warfare.*

The stormy weather had also forced Weddigen to take *U9* below the surface. His original mission had been to attack British transports at Ostend, but when he broke surface again and sighted the three cruisers, he realized that this was too good a target to ignore.

THE SINKING OF *ABOUKIR*

At 0620 the *U9* fired a single torpedo at the nearest cruiser, *Aboukir*, hitting her on the starboard side, flooding the engine room, and forcing her to stop immediately. No submarines had been sighted, so *Aboukir*'s captain assumed that the warship had struck a mine and therefore ordered the other two cruisers to close in and help. Because of damage caused by the explosion and the failure of the steam winches needed to launch the lifeboats, only one got away. *Aboukir* capsized, and sank five minutes later.

Weddigen fired two more torpedoes at his next target, *Hogue*, from a range of only 886 ft (270 m). As the torpedoes left the submarine, her bows rose out of the water and she was spotted by the *Hogue*, which opened fire before Weddigen was able to dive again. Then his torpedoes struck the warship, which capsized and sank after 10 minutes.

At 0720 Weddigen launched two torpedoes from her stern tubes at *Cressy*. One missed, so he turned the boat and fired his one remaining bow tube from 550 yards (500 m). The stern tube torpedo struck *Cressy*'s starboard side, the other her port beam. She capsized and floated upside-down for some time before sinking.

In improving weather, rescue vessels picked up 837 men from the three British warships, but 1,459 lost their lives. Weddigen evaded British destroyers and escaped on the surface. His reputation was enhanced when, three weeks later, he sank the old cruiser *Hawke* off Aberdeen.

U29

In 1915, Weddigen, by now highly decorated, had been appointed to command a more modern submarine, designated *U29*. On March 18, she was rammed and sunk off the Moray Firth, Scotland, by the battleship *Dreadnought*. There were no survivors.

The *U9*, having been withdrawn from first-line service and given a training role, survived the war and was surrendered to the British in November 1918. She was broken up at Morecambe the following year.

Of her sisters, *U11* was mined and sunk in the Dover Straits on December 12, 1914; *U12* was rammed and sunk in the North Sea by the destroyer *Ariel* on March 10, 1915; and *U10* was mined and sunk in the Baltic on May 27, 1916.

Derfflinger 1913

The battlecruiser *Derfflinger* and her sisters, *Hindenburg* and *Lutzöw*, were arguably the finest capital ships of their day, their design providing the basis for future German warships. *Derfflinger* was named after Field Marshal Baron Georg von Derfflinger (1606–95) of Brandenburg.

CREW
The usual crew for a *Derfflinger*-class ship was 44 officers and 1,086 men, but when serving as a flagship for the 1st Scouting Group, they carried an additional 14 officers and 62 men.

ARMAMENT
The *Derfflinger* class of ships were fitted with 12-in (305-mm) guns, and were the only German battlecruisers to carry this caliber of main armament. They were easily distinguishable from earlier German battlecruisers in that their turrets were all on the centerline in superfiring (superimposed) pairs aligned fore and aft.

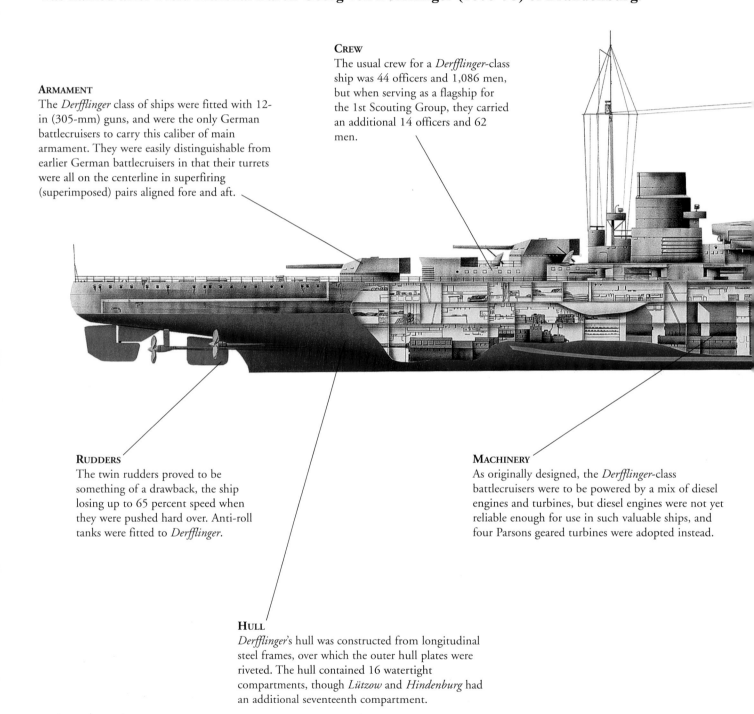

RUDDERS
The twin rudders proved to be something of a drawback, the ship losing up to 65 percent speed when they were pushed hard over. Anti-roll tanks were fitted to *Derfflinger*.

MACHINERY
As originally designed, the *Derfflinger*-class battlecruisers were to be powered by a mix of diesel engines and turbines, but diesel engines were not yet reliable enough for use in such valuable ships, and four Parsons geared turbines were adopted instead.

HULL
Derfflinger's hull was constructed from longitudinal steel frames, over which the outer hull plates were riveted. The hull contained 16 watertight compartments, though *Lützow* and *Hindenburg* had an additional seventeenth compartment.

ARMOR
In general, German battlecruisers were better protected than their British counterparts, but they did not sacrifice speed for armor. Their designers used lighter machinery and a lighter hull construction.

DERFFLINGER – SPECIFICATION

Country of origin: Germany
Type: Battlecruiser
Laid down: March 30, 1912
Builder: Blohm & Voss, Hamburg
Launched: July 17, 1913
Commissioned: September 1, 1914
Fate: Scuttled in Scapa Flow on June 21, 1919
Complement: 44 officers and 1,068 men

Dimensions:
Displacement (normal load): 28,860 tons (26,180 tonnes)
Displacement (full load): 24,400 tons (31,200 tonnes)
Length: 690 ft (210 m); **Beam:** 95 ft (29 m);

Draught: 30.2 ft (9.2 m)

Power plant:
Propulsion: 4 shaft Parsons turbines; 18 boilers; 76,634 shp
Speed: 26.5 knots
Range: 5,600 nmi (10,371km) at 12 knots

Armor & Armament:
Armor: 1.2–12 in (30–300 mm)
Armament: 8 x 12-in (305-mm) SK L/50 in 4 twin turrets;
12 x 5.9-in (150-mm) SK L/45 in 12 single turrets;
4 x 3.5-in (88-mm) in 4 single mounts; 4 x single 20-in (500-mm) torpedo tubes

The Battle of Jutland, in which *Derfflinger* was
heavily engaged, marked the beginning of the
end for the German High Seas Fleet. This
formidable German force retreated to its main
base at Wilhelmshaven, and never ventured out
in strength again. The two ships shown here were
both involved in the Battle of Jutland.

GERMAN BATTLECRUISER*: MOLTKE*

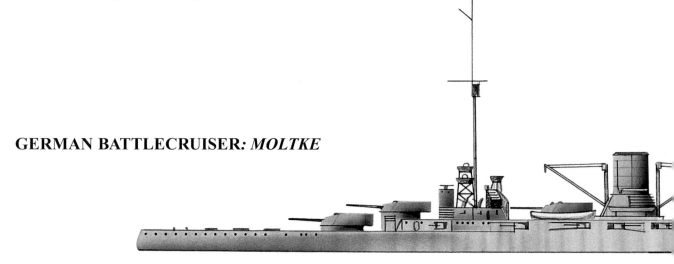

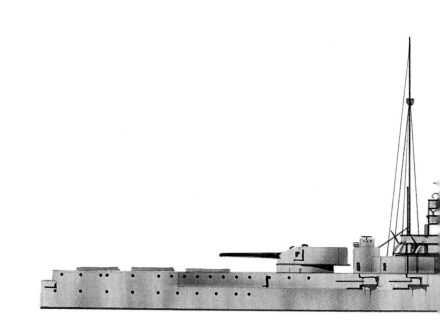

DERFFLINGER

Built by Blohm & Voss at their yard in Hamburg, *Derfflinger*'s keel was laid in January 1912. She was to have been launched on June 14, 1913, but the wooden sledges upon which the ship rested became jammed and the ship moved only 12–16 in (30–40 cm). A second attempt was successful on July 12, 1913. A crew composed of dockyard workers took the ship around the Skagen to Kiel. In late October, the vessel was assigned to the 1st Scouting Group, but damage to the ship's turbines during trials prevented her from joining the unit until November 16.

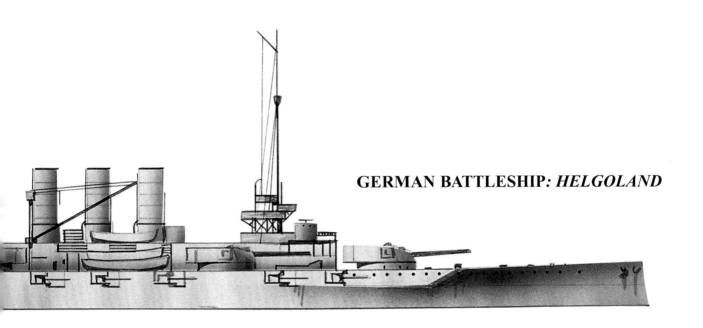

GERMAN BATTLESHIP: *HELGOLAND*

The raids on English coastal towns by *Derfflinger* and other units of the German Navy caused outrage among the British public. The attacks killed many innocent men, women, and children, giving rise to furious demands for revenge.

In the early morning of December 16, 1914, the German battlecruisers *Seydlitz*, *Moltke*, and *Blücher* bombarded West Hartlepool, while *Derfflinger* and *Von der Tann* shelled Scarborough and Whitby, killing 127 civilians and injuring 567. *Moltke* and *Blücher* were hit by shore batteries but all the raiders escaped in the mist.

The Royal Navy's 1st Battlecruiser Squadron under Admiral Beatty and the 2nd Battle Squadron under Admiral Warrender were already at sea to intercept the attackers, which were sighted on their approach to the coast by British destroyers. At 0445 the latter were engaged by the German cruiser *Hamburg* and escorting light forces, which disabled the destroyer *Hardy* and damaged *Ambuscade* and *Lynx*. During the early part of the day the German battlecruisers, returning from their attack, passed some miles astern of the 2nd Battle Squadron, which sighted the German ships and turned to close with them, only to be thwarted by bad weather and ambiguous signals from Beatty, which led to the light cruisers breaking off the chase. A golden opportunity was lost.

Close-up

Derfflinger suffered serious damage at the Battle of Jutland, but her armor enabled her to avoid the same fate as befell the British battlecruisers.

(1) **Size:** *Derfflinger* was the largest and most powerful German battlecruiser of her time.

(2) **Damage:** The battle scars inflicted on *Derfflinger* at Jutland are clearly visible in this photograph. Her stubborn resistance earned her the nickname "Iron Dog."

(3) **Superstructure:** *Derfflinger*'s superstructure was well designed, and set a trend for the construction of later battlecruisers.

(4) **Derrick:** After she was repaired after the Battle of Jutland, *Derfflinger* carried out experiments with seaplanes, a derrick being mounted amidships.

(5) **Hits:** *Derfflinger* took 21 shell hits at Jutland, with 157 of her crew killed. Many more were wounded, but managed to survive.

(6) **Armor:** Four 3.5-in (88-mm) Flak guns were installed amidships. The ship also carried four 20-in (500-mm) submerged torpedo tubes.

Clouds of dense black smoke billow out over the sea as Derfflinger *fires a broadside. Her gunnery was extremely accurate, and reflected the high standard of training in the German Navy.*

Another opportunity was squandered on January 24, 1915, when the Germans set out on an offensive sweep of the southeastern Dogger Bank. Decoded radio intercepts had given the British advance knowledge that a German raiding squadron was heading for Dogger Bank, so they dispatched their own naval forces to intercept it. The British found the Germans at the expected time and place; surprised, the smaller and slower German squadron fled for home. During a stern chase lasting several hours, the British slowly caught up with the Germans and engaged them with long-range gunfire. The British disabled the *Blücher*, at the rear of the German line, but the Germans put the British flagship (HMS *Lion*) out of action with heavy damage. Due to signalling errors, the remaining British ships broke off pursuit of the fleeing enemy force and returned to sink the crippled *Blücher*. By the time they had finished her off, the German squadron had escaped; all the remaining German vessels returned safely to harbor, though some, including the *Derfflinger*, had sustained heavy damage.

REPAIRED IN TIME FOR BATTLE

She was repaired in time to take part in the Battle of Jutland on May 31, 1916, when she formed part of the German battlecruiser squadron, which also included *Lützow*, *Moltke*, *Seydlitz*, and *Von der Tann*. At 1630 that afternoon, the *Lion*-class battlecruiser *Queen Mary* took a direct hit from the *Derfflinger* and blew up with a tremendous explosion. There were only nine survivors out of her crew of 1266.

Later, *Derfflinger* was also to play a part in sinking the British battlecruiser *Invincible*, but she herself was badly damaged in the battle, sustaining 21 shell hits, with 157 of her crew dead. Her sister ship, *Lützow*, was also heavily damaged, with 116 of her crew killed. Unable to make it back to Wilhelmshaven, she was sunk by a German destroyer.

In November 1918, after the Armistice, *Derfflinger* was interned at Scapa Flow in the Orkney Islands, and on June 21, 1919 she was scuttled there by her crew. She was raised and broken up at Rosyth in 1934.

Hood 1918

The battlecruiser *Hood* was the very symbol of Empire, of power and majesty, underlining the fact that the *Pax Britannica* was still in force and that Britain continued to rule much of the world. At 42,000 tons (38,000 tonnes) she was the mightiest warship afloat.

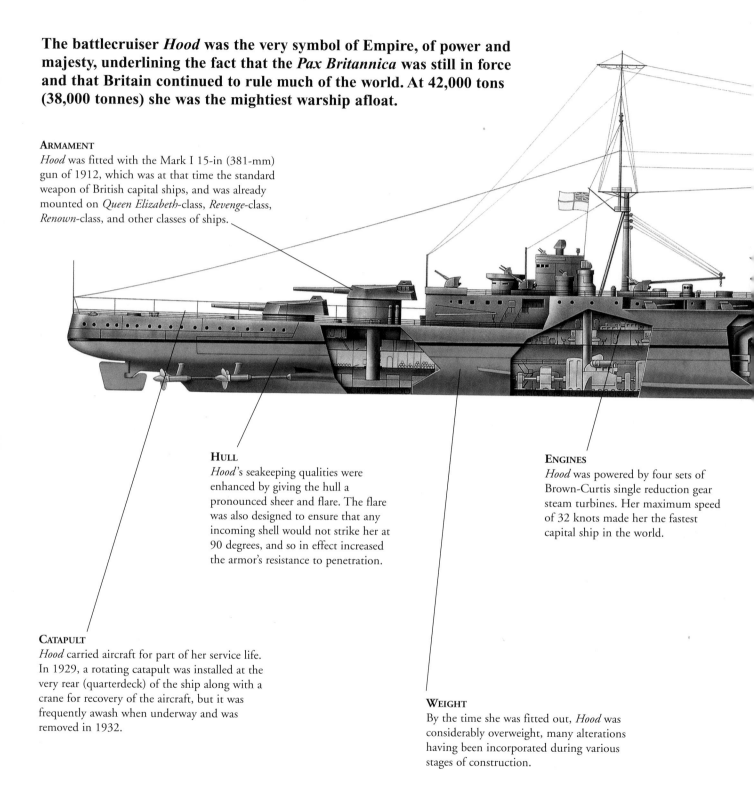

ARMAMENT
Hood was fitted with the Mark I 15-in (381-mm) gun of 1912, which was at that time the standard weapon of British capital ships, and was already mounted on *Queen Elizabeth*-class, *Revenge*-class, *Renown*-class, and other classes of ships.

HULL
Hood's seakeeping qualities were enhanced by giving the hull a pronounced sheer and flare. The flare was also designed to ensure that any incoming shell would not strike her at 90 degrees, and so in effect increased the armor's resistance to penetration.

ENGINES
Hood was powered by four sets of Brown-Curtis single reduction gear steam turbines. Her maximum speed of 32 knots made her the fastest capital ship in the world.

CATAPULT
Hood carried aircraft for part of her service life. In 1929, a rotating catapult was installed at the very rear (quarterdeck) of the ship along with a crane for recovery of the aircraft, but it was frequently awash when underway and was removed in 1932.

WEIGHT
By the time she was fitted out, *Hood* was considerably overweight, many alterations having been incorporated during various stages of construction.

- Launched August 22, 1918, completed March 1920.

- World Cruise, 1923–24.

- Mediterranean, 1936–38.

- Refit 1940, anti-aircraft armament increased.

- Sunk by German battleship *Bismarck* in Denmark Strait, May 24, 1941, with 1,416 dead, and three survivors.

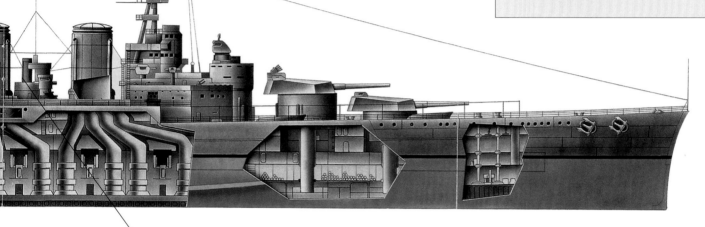

ARMOR
Hood's biggest flaw was her armor. The deck and side armor failed to provide continuous protection against shells coming in from all angles.

HOOD – SPECIFICATION

Country of origin: United Kingdom
Type: "Admiral"-class Battlecruiser
Laid down: September 1, 1916
Builder: John Brown & Company
Launched: August 22, 1918
Commissioned: May 15, 1920
Decommissioned: n/a
Fate: Sunk in combat May 24, 1941
Complement: (1921) 1168; (1941) 1419

Dimensions:
Displacement: 42,000 tons (38,000 tonnes)
Length: 860 ft 7 in (262.3 m); **Beam:** 104 ft 2 in (31.75 m);
Draught: 32 ft (9.75 m)

Power plant:
Propulsion: Quadruple screw Brown-Curtis geared steam
   turbines
Speed: 32 knots
Range: (1931) 9,875 (5,332 nm) at 20 knots

Armament & Armor:
Armament: (as built) 8 x BL 15-in (381-mm) Mk I guns;
   12 x 5.5-in (140-mm) Mk I guns; 4 4-in (102-mm) Mark V
   anti-aircraft guns; 6 x 21-in (533-mm) Mark IV torpedo tubes
Armor: 0.75–12 in (19–305 mm)

Hood was an enlarged *Queen Elizabeth*-type, and was designed in response to the planned German *Mackensen*-class battlecruisers. Her original design was modified because of lessons learned during the Battle of Jutland, but she remained poorly protected.

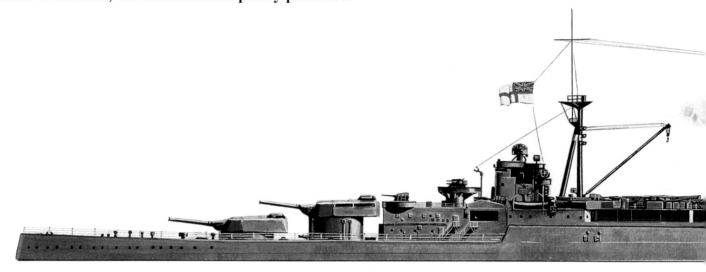

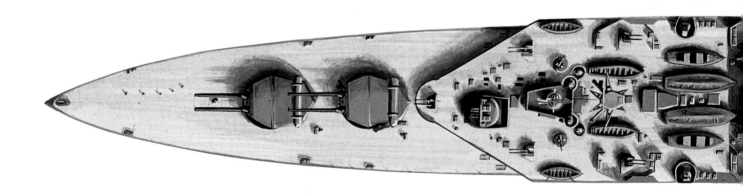

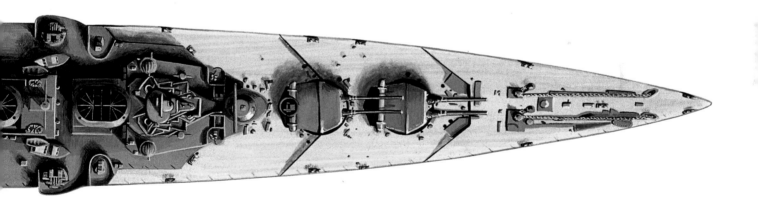

HOOD

Hood was the name of several distinguished British Admirals, the first of whom, Viscount Hood, served with distinction under Admiral Rodney during the eighteenth-century wars with France. His brother, Alexander Hood, 1st Viscount Bridport, was also an admiral, while Rear-Admiral Sir Samuel Hood, his cousin once removed, commanded the warship *Zealous* at the Battle of the Nile. The last of the line, Rear-Admiral Horace Hood, commanded the 3rd Battlecruiser Squadron at the Battle of Jutland in 1916 and was lost when his flagship, *Invincible*, exploded. It was his widow who launched the mighty *Hood* two years later.

"The mist lifted to reveal the *Hood* and her consorts coming in…. It was a wonderful sight, something I shall never forget, everyone cheering and the kids running up and down and the sirens of all the ships in the harbor going off." (Eyewitness account of *Hood*'s visit to Melbourne, Australia)

In November 1923, accompanied by the battlecruiser *Repulse* and five cruisers, *Hood* embarked on a year-long world tour. The itinerary took her and her consorts to South Africa, Zanzibar, Ceylon, Singapore, Australia, New Zealand, the Pacific Islands, San Francisco, the Panama Canal, Jamaica, and finally Newfoundland. The powerful naval squadron attracted huge crowds wherever it dropped anchor.

A LONG REFIT

But *Hood*'s true purpose was warfare, and in May 1929 she was laid up for a long refit, emerging in June 1930 with

Interior view

Like most other warships of the time, *Hood* carried an armament of torpedoes. These consisted of six 21-in (533-mm) torpedo tubes in her case mounted amidships, three on either side.

(1) **Stowage:** The torpedo room held stowage racks for storing, maintaining, and loading the ship's torpedoes.

(2) **Torpedo motor:** The aft end of the torpedo contained the motor. Some torpedoes were powered by steam, but most had powerful electric motors.

(3) **Components:** Every rotating component had a matching component that turned in the opposite direction, preventing unbalanced torques (twisting forces).

(4) **Usage:** Naval strategy in *Hood*'s time was to use torpedoes launched from submarines or warships, as part of a fleet action on the high seas.

(5) **Detonation:** To avoid a warship's armored belt, torpedoes were often set to detonate underneath a ship, where they did maximum damage to its keel.

(6) **Storage racks:** Neatness was essential in the crowded space of a torpedo room, so storage racks had to be well organized.

Because of flaws in her design, it was seriously suggested that Hood *should be scrapped before she was launched, a fate that overtook her planned sister ships. However,* Hood *was too far advanced and cancellation would have cost too much.*

modifications that included the installation of a catapult for launching a spotter aircraft and a recovery crane. This was installed at the rear of the quarterdeck, but was frequently awash when the ship was travelling at full speed, and it was removed in 1932.

Hood continued to serve with the Home and Atlantic fleets until 1936, when she sailed to join the Mediterranean Fleet. In September 1938 she suffered damage when she ran aground at Gibraltar, and in the following year she went in for another refit, which involved a substantial increase in her anti-aircraft armament.

THE ROYAL NAVY'S FINEST

Her status as the Royal Navy's finest capital ship meant that she was almost constantly in active service, and by the end of the 1930s her condition was beginning to deteriorate badly. As a result her performance suffered. Among other things, she was unable to attain her maximum design speed. In 1939 she was once again serving with the Home Fleet, the flagship of the Battle Cruiser Squadron at Scapa Flow, and when war broke out in September that year she was employed principally in patrolling the vicinity of Iceland and the Faeroes to protect convoys and intercept German raiders attempting to break out into the Atlantic. In September 1939,

she was hit by a 550-lb (250-kg) aircraft bomb and sustained minor damage. As the flagship of Force H, she took part in the destruction of the French Fleet at Mers-el-Kebir in July 1940. In August, she rejoined the Battle Cruiser Squadron and resumed patrolling against German raiders.

She was due to be fully modernized in 1941, to bring her up to the standard of other capital ships built during World War I, but the outbreak of war meant that it was impossible to remove her from service. Consequently she never received the required update. That update was to have included the addition of full deck armor.

On May 24, 1941, together with the battleship *Prince of Wales*, she engaged the German battleship *Bismarck* and the heavy cruiser *Prinz Eugen* in the Denmark Strait. The *Bismarck*'s second and third salvoes struck the battlecruiser amidships, and those from the *Prinz Eugen* started a fire among her ready-to-use AA ammunition. At 0600, as the British warships were altering course in order to bring all their guns to bear, *Hood* was hit again by a salvo that pierced her lightly armored decks and detonated in her after magazines. She blew up with a tremendous explosion and disappeared with a speed that astounded all who witnessed the event. Only three of her crew of 1,419 officers and seamen survived.

Scharnhorst 1936

The design of *Scharnhorst* and her sister, *Gneisenau*, was based on that of the uncompleted *Mackensen-class* battlecruisers of World War I, which in turn were based on the *Derfflinger* of 1913, arguably the best battlecruiser of its day. The two warships represented a powerful threat to Allied Atlantic convoys.

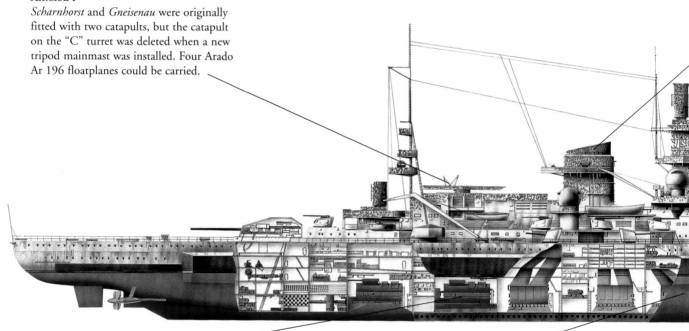

AIRCRAFT
Scharnhorst and *Gneisenau* were originally fitted with two catapults, but the catapult on the "C" turret was deleted when a new tripod mainmast was installed. Four Arado Ar 196 floatplanes could be carried.

MACHINERY
Scharnhorst was powered by three Brown-Boveri geared turbines with 12 Wagner boilers, producing 165,000 shp (123.09 MW) and giving a top speed of 32 knots and a range of 8,800 nm (16,298 km) at 16 knots.

ARMOR
The adoption of the 11-in (280-mm) armament meant that more protection could be carried without any appreciable weight penalty. The main belt was 12–13 in (305–330 mm), turrets 12 in (305 mm), and decks 6 in (152 mm).

SCHARNHORST – SPECIFICATION

Country of origin: Germany
Type: Battlecruiser
Laid down: 1935
Builder: Deutsche Werke, Kriegsmarinewerft Wilhelmshaven
Launched: Late 1936
Commissioned: Early 1939
Decommissioned: n/a
Fate: Sunk in Battle of North Cape, December 26, 1943
Complement: 1,968 (56 officers, 1,909 enlisted)

Dimensions:
Displacement: (standard) 35,952 tons (32,615 tonnes); (full load) 42,672 tons (34,564 tonnes)

Length: (overall) 772 ft (235 m); (waterline) 741.5 ft (226 m);
Beam: 98.4 ft (30 m); **Draught:** 31 ft 9 in (9.69 m)

Power plant:
Propulsion: 12 Wagner boilers, producing 165,000 shp (123.09 MW)
Speed: 32 knots
Range: 8,800 nm (16,298 km) at 16 knots

Armament & Armor:
Armament: 9 x 11-in (280-mm) guns; 12 x 5.9-in (150-mm) guns
Armor: 3.7–13.78 in (95–350 mm)
Aircraft: 4 Arado Ar 196A-3

FACTS

- Launched October 3, 1936; completed January 1939.

- Sinks British auxiliary cruiser *Rawalpindi*, November 1939.

- Operations off Norway, April–June 1940; sinks aircraft carrier *Glorious* and destroyers *Ardent* and *Acasta*, June 8, 1940. Damaged in torpedo attack by *Acasta*.

- Sortie into North Atlantic with *Gneisenau*, January–March 1941. Sinks 22 ships.

- Damaged by air attack at La Pallice, July 1941.

- Damaged by mines in English Channel during "Channel Dash," February 1942.

- Sunk in action with *Duke of York* off North Cape, Norway, December 26, 1943 (1,932 dead).

SUPERSTRUCTURE
The mainmast was originally immediately aft of the funnel, but was moved farther back in 1939. A funnel cap was also added.

BOW
Scharnhorst's original straight stem was altered to a "clipper bow" in 1939, making her a more satisfactory seaboat.

MAIN ARMAMENT
Hitler ordered that *Scharnhorst* and *Gneisenau* were to be fitted with 15-in (380-mm) guns, but as the 11-in (280-mm) triple turret was readily available the warships were fitted with this instead. Plans to install the heavier armament at a later date were abandoned.

Scharnhorst and *Gneisenau* presented a dire threat to the vital Allied Atlantic convoys. Had they been able to form a battle group with the German battleship *Bismarck* and the heavy cruiser *Prinz Eugen,* they would have been virtually invincible.

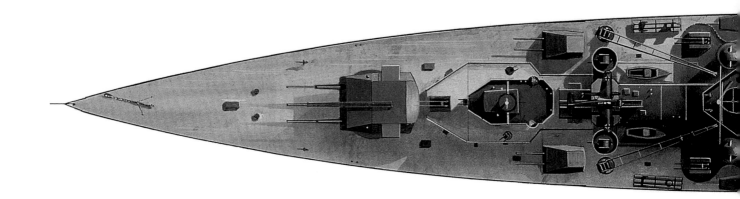

SISTER SHIP: *GNEISENAU*

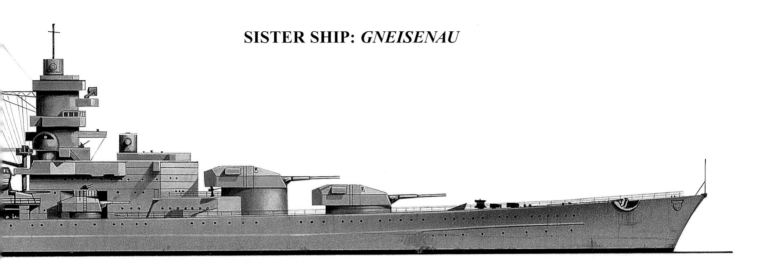

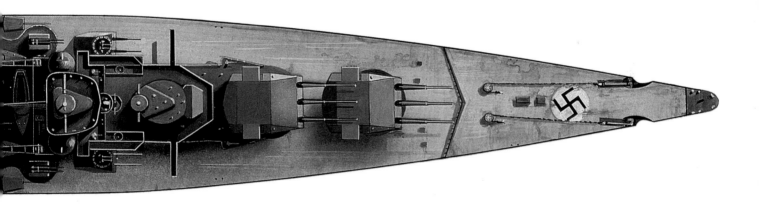

DESTROYING *SCHARNHORST* AND *GNIESENAU*

In 1941, the Royal Air Force made determined efforts to destroy *Scharnhorst* and *Gneisenau* in their bases on the French Atlantic coast. On July 24, 15 Halifax bombers made a daylight attack on *Scharnhorst* at La Pallice; five direct hits were scored, but three bombs passed straight through the ship and the other two failed to explode. Five of the Halifaxes were shot down and all the rest damaged. However, the damage they managed to inflict on *Scharnhorst* was enough to put her out of action for four months.

"The *Scharnhorst* must have been a hell on earth. The 14-inch from the flagship were hitting or rocketing off from a ricochet on the sea. Great flashes rent the night, and the sound of gunfire was continuous, and yet she replied, but only occasionally now with what armament she had left."

– LT B.B. RAMSDEN.

Those words, by Lieutenant B.B. Ramsden, an officer of Royal Marines on the British battleship *Duke of York*, described the end of *Scharnhorst* on a freezing December night off Norway's North Cape. She had been a thorn in the side of the Royal Navy since 1940, when she sank the aircraft carrier *Glorious* and the destroyers *Ardent* and *Acasta* off Norway on June 8.

Commerce raiding was her main role, and early in 1941 *Scharnhorst* and *Gneisenau* sank 22 Allied ships totaling 115,622 tons (104,890 tonnes) on a sortie into the North Atlantic, before seeking refuge in the French Atlantic ports. There they were joined by the heavy cruiser *Prinz Eugen* after the latter's consort, the battleship *Bismarck*, was sunk at the end of May. In February 1942, repaired after sustaining varying degrees of damage sustained in RAF air attacks, the three warships made an epic dash through the English Channel and reached the safety of Kiel. *Gneisenau*

Close-up

The *Scharnhorst* and her sister ship *Gneisenau* were extremely well equipped, with plenty of room below decks. This is the engine room.

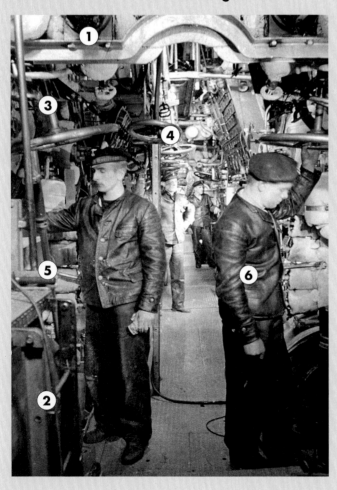

1. **Machinery:** After her commerce-raiding expeditions in the Atlantic, *Scharnhorst*'s machinery needed a lengthy overhaul.

2. **Main machinery:** This was a triple-shaft steam turbine arrangement with 12 Wagner high-pressure boilers, three in each of four boiler rooms.

3. **Cruising turbines:** These were fitted initially but removed later. The after turbine room powered the center shaft.

4. **Battlecruiser or battleship:** Although the British referred to *Scharnhorst* and *Gneisenau* as battlecruisers, the Germans always described them as battleships.

5. **Armor:** This was equal to that of a battleship, and if it had not been for her small-caliber guns, she would have been classified as a battleship by the British.

6. **Gallantry:** After *Scharnhorst*'s last battle, her crew were complimented by the British Admiral Bruce Fraser, who told his officers: "I hope that if any of you are ever called upon to lead a ship into action against an opponent many times superior, you will command your ship as gallantly as *Scharnhorst* was commanded today."

The German Navy's Commander Battleships, Vice-Admiral Ciliax, inspects the crew of Scharnhorst, *accompanied by Captain Hoffman (right) and executive officers. Together,* Scharnhorst, Gneisenau, *and* Prinz Eugen *made a formidable battle group.*

was hit by Bomber Command in Kiel harbor two weeks later and never went to sea again; her gun turrets were removed for coastal defense and she was sunk as a blockship at Gdynia, where she was seized by the Russians and broken up from 1947–51. Only *Scharnhorst* re-emerged to threaten Allied shipping on the high seas, her base now in Norway.

FINISHED OFF BY BRITAIN

At 1400 on December 25, 1943, *Scharnhorst* (Captain F. Hintze, flying the flag of Admiral Bey) sailed from Norway accompanied by five destroyers to intercept Convoy JW55B, which had been located by air reconnaissance on December 22. She was intercepted by a force of British cruisers and destroyers, and damaged by their gunfire.

Her fate was sealed by the arrival of the battleship *Duke of York*, which opened fire on her and put the battlecruiser's "A" and "B" turrets out of action. Some steam pipes were also ruptured. This reduced her speed, leaving her without

the capability of outrunning her adversaries, even if the opportunity had arisen.

At 1824 the third of *Scharnhorst*'s turrets was put out of action, and British destroyers moved in to finish the job. Two of them, *Savage* and *Saumarez*, approached from the northwest under heavy fire, firing starshell, while *Scorpion* and *Stord* attacked fom the southeast, launching their torpedoes at 1849. As Hintze turned his ship to port to engage them, one of *Scorpion*'s torpedoes struck home, closely followed by three more from the first two destroyers.

A CHALLENGE THAT FAILED

By 1930 the battlecruiser was ablaze, her hull glowing red-hot in the Arctic night. Destroyers closed in to finish her off with torpedoes. At 1945 she blew up. Only 36 of her crew of 1,968 were rescued from the freezing seas. So ended the Battle of North Cape, and with it the last attempt by a German capital ship to challenge the supremacy of the Royal Navy.

Enterprise (CV-6) 1936

The first U.S. carrier built from the keel up was the *Ranger* of 1930, which proved too slow to be effective as a first-line unit. She was, however, developed into the successful *Yorktown* class of 1933 (which included *Enterprise*, *Hornet*, and *Yorktown*), followed by *Wasp* of 1934.

ARMAMENT
By the end of the war, in addition to her eight 5-in (127-mm) guns, *Enterprise* had 11 quadruple 1.57-in (40-mm) guns, 8 twin 1.79-in (40-mm) guns, and 16 twin 0.79-in (20-mm) anti-aircraft weapons.

HANGARS
The aircraft hangars were light structures independent of the hull, and could be closed off with rolling shutters. The three lifts were completely enclosed by the flight deck.

MACHINERY
Four Curtis and Parsons geared turbines produced 120,000 shp (89,520 MW), giving the *Yorktown*-class ships a maximum speed of 34 knots. *Endurance* was 8,220 nm (15,223 km), at 20 knots.

FLIGHT DECK
The early design of the *Yorktown* class envisaged a flush flight deck with horizontal funnels, but this was thought to pose a smoke hazard to landing aircraft. Instead, the carriers were fitted with an island to carry funnel uptakes and provide space for control centers.

PROTECTION

For a time, an armored flight deck was considered, but not enough armor could be provided for this to be useful without sacrificing speed. As a result, the deck carried only 3 in (76 mm) of armor plate.

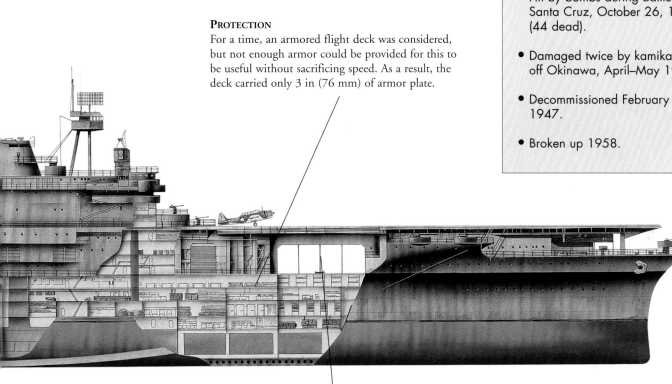

AIRCRAFT

The *Yorktown*-class carriers could carry and operate up to 80 aircraft. A hangar deck catapult was installed in all three ships, but was removed from *Enterprise* and *Hornet* in 1942.

ENTERPRISE (CV-6) – SPECIFICATION

Country of origin: USA
Type: Aircraft carrier
Laid down: July 16, 1934
Builder: Newport News Shipbuilding
Launched: October 3, 1936
Commissioned: May 12, 1938
Decommissioned: February 17, 1947
Fate: Scrapped 1958–60
Complement: 2,217

Dimensions:
Displacement: (standard) 19,800 tons (17,962 tonnes), (full load) 25,500 tons (23,133 tonnes)
Length: 770 ft (230 m) (waterline); 824 ft 9 in (251 m) (overall)
Beam: 83 ft 3 in (25 m); 109 ft 6 in (33.38 m) (overall)

Draught: 25 ft 11.5 in (7.912 m)

Power plant:
Propulsion: 4 shaft geared system turbines delivering 120,000 shp (89.520 MW)
Speed: 34 knots
Range: 8,220 nm (15,223 km)

Armament & Armor:
Armament: 8 x 5-in (127-mm) guns
Armor: 2.5–4 in (63.5–101.6 mm)
Aircraft: 80

At the time of the Japanese attack on Pearl Harbor, *Enterprise* was at sea about 200 miles (320 km) west of Hawaii returning from Wake Island after delivering a Marine fighter squadron. Together with *Lexington*, *Yorktown*, and *Saratoga*, she would form the nucleus of a rebuilt Pacific Fleet.

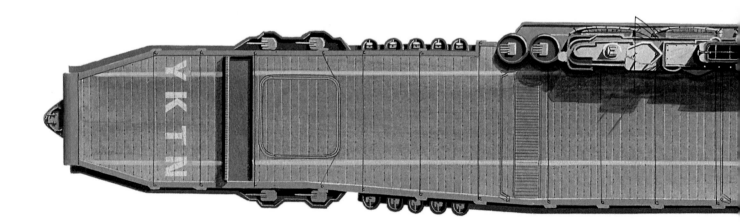

SISTER SHIP: *YORKTOWN*

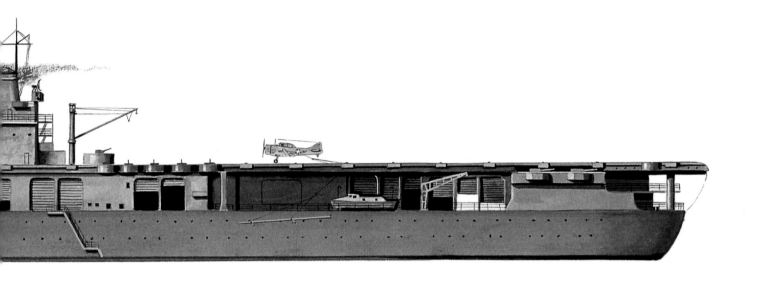

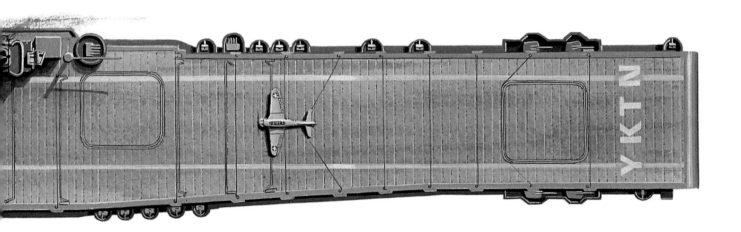

YORKTOWN CLASS

Although the four carriers of the U.S. Pacific Fleet escaped the Pearl Harbor attack, losses came more quickly than reinforcements could be redeployed from the Atlantic. The *Yorktown* was damaged by bombs in the Battle of Midway on June 5, 1942, and was finished off by a Japanese submarine two days later. The third of the *Yorktown* class, *Hornet*, had only just been completed in December 1941; her first action, in April 1942, was to launch a force of B-25 Mitchell bombers in the famous "Doolittle Raid" on Tokyo. She was sunk at the Battle of Santa Cruz in October that year.

It would be no exaggeration to claim that *Enterprise* was the hardest-worked carrier of World War II. She fought in almost every Pacific campaign, and withstood terrible damage in enemy air attacks.

Six months after Pearl Harbor, a crushing humiliation was about to descend on the hitherto invincible Japanese Navy. Early in June 1942, the four carriers that had taken part in the Pearl Harbor attack – *Akagi, Kaga, Hiryu,* and *Soryu* – formed part of the strong naval force that was intended to bombard the island of Midway into submission prior to a Japanese landing and occupation, a crucial step in Admiral Yamamoto's plan to expand the perimeter of Japan's conquest eastwards towards the continental United States, which would then come under direct threat.

The thrust towards Midway was met by a greatly outnumbered U.S. carrier force composed of Rear Admiral Fletcher's Task Force 17, with *Yorktown,* and Rear Admiral R.A. Spruance's Task Force 16, with *Hornet* and *Enterprise,* supported by Navy, Marine Corps and Army air units based on Midway.

Close-up

Enterprise participated in more major actions of the war against Japan than any other U.S. warship. On three occasions during the Pacific War, the Japanese announced she had been sunk in action.

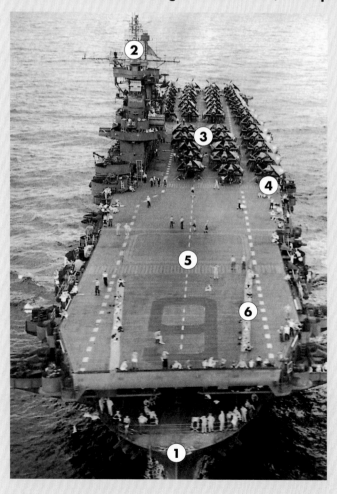

(1) In motion: *Enterprise* steams towards the Panama Canal on October 10, 1945, en route to New York to participate in Navy Day celebrations.

(2) Superstructure: *Enterprise* had a traditional design for the time, with her superstructure, or "island," situated on the starboard side.

(3) Flight deck: Three aircraft lifts provided access to the flight deck. A single hangar deck catapult was fitted with twin flight deck catapults, all three hydraulically powered.

(4) Complement: *Enterprise* had a complement of 2,217 personnel and could field 90 aircraft of various types including fighters, dive bombers and torpedo bombers.

(5) Engine: *Enterprise* was powered by nine Babcock and Wilcox boilers servicing four Parsons geared turbines, turning four shafts with an output of 120,000 shp (89.52 MW)

(6) Armor: *Enterprise's* flight deck had 3 in (76 mm) of armor plating, about twice the thickness of other U.S. aircraft carriers. It was to save her life more than once.

Enterprise is pictured here during her early years of service with the U.S. Fleet. The aircraft on her deck are Grumman F3F biplane fighters. She went on to participate in many major actions of war.

At 0700 on June 4 *Enterprise* and *Hornet* launched their strike groups. *Enterprise*'s air group attacked *Soryu* with 12 TBDs of VT-3 and 17 SBDs of VB-3. Only five TBDs survived to make their torpedo attacks, and three of these were shot down on the way out. Of the 41 TBDs launched, only six returned to the task force, and one of these ran out of fuel and ditched.

JAPANESE SHIPS GO DOWN

The sacrifice of the three VT squadrons was not in vain. They had absorbed the bulk of the enemy fighter attacks, and the Japanese fighters were still scattered when 37 Dauntless dive-bombers from *Enterprise*'s VB-5 and the 17 from *Yorktown*'s VB-3 made their attack, sinking the *Akagi*, *Kaga*, and *Soryu*. The cost to the dive-bombers was 16 aircraft lost from *Enterprise*'s air group. A Japanese counterattack from *Hiryu* damaged *Yorktown*, but she returned to full operation after a short time. Then a second attack was made by six B5N Kate torpedo-bombers. Two were shot down, but the other four launched their torpedoes and two hit the carrier, which had to be abandoned. She was later sunk by a submarine. At 1700, *Hiryu* was

crippled in an attack by 24 SBDs from *Enterprise*. Her burnt-out hulk was sunk by a Japanese destroyer the following day. In August 1942, *Enterprise* was severely damaged by bombs during the Battle of the Eastern Solomons. Repaired at Pearl Harbor, she returned to action in October only to be damaged again. Repair work was still incomplete when she saw further action in December during the battle for Guadalcanal during the Battle of Rennell Island.

OVERHAULED AT LAST

More action in 1943 saw *Enterprise* receive a Presidential Unit Citation, the first awarded to an aircraft carrier. In July, relieved at last by the new *Essex*-class carriers, she returned to the USA for a badly needed overhaul.

Enterprise went on to gain more battle honors, her air group participating in the Battle of the Philippine Sea and striking at Palau, Leyte, Luzon, Formosa, the China coast, Iwo Jima, and Okinawa. In addition, she survived two kamikaze attacks off Okinawa.

She was scrapped in 1958, despite efforts to preserve her as a memorial.

Cossack 1937

Among the finest destroyers ever built for the Royal Navy, the 16 "Tribal"-class vessels, of which *Cossack* was one, were produced as a counter to those being built by potential enemies, rather than to fill any clearly definable role within the fleet.

ARMAMENT
Because they were intended primarily to counter vessels like the Japanese *Fubuki*-class super destroyers, the "Tribals" carried a heavy armament of four twin 4.7–in (120-mm) guns and one quadruple 21-in (533-mm) torpedo mounting.

HULL
By any standards the "Tribal" class were magnificent ships to look at, their pleasingly balanced profile in harmony with the high freeboard hull that was introduced to improve their fighting qualities in poor weather.

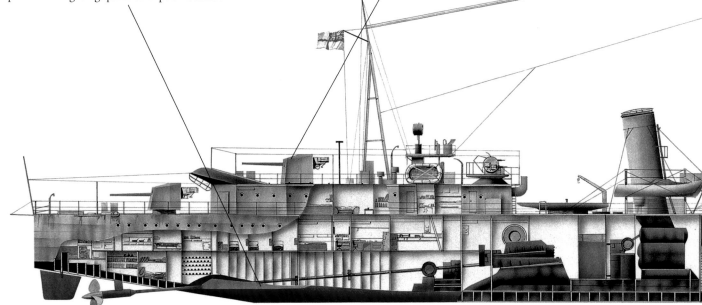

COSSACK – SPECIFICATION

Country of origin: United Kingdom
Type: Destroyer
Laid down: June 9, 1936
Builder: Vickers-Armstrongs at Newcastle-on-Tyne, England
Launched: June 8, 1937
Commissioned: June 7, 1938
Fate: Sunk October 27, 1941
Complement: 219

Dimensions:
Displacement: 1,870 tons (1,696 tonnes)
Length: 364 ft 8 in (111.5 m); **Beam:** 36 ft 6 in (11.13 m);
 Draught: 13 ft (4 m)

Power plant:
Propulsion: 2 shaft Parsons geared turbines developing 44,000 shp (33,131 kW)
Speed: 36 knots

Armament & Armor:
Armament: 8 x 4.7-in (120-mm) twin turrets; 1 x quadruple 2-lb (0.9-kg) anti-aircraft guns; 2 x quadruple 0.5in (12.7-mm) caliber MGs; 1 x quadruple torpedo tubes (21-in [533-mm] Mk IX Torpedoes); 2 x Depth charge throwers; 1 x Depth charge rail
Armor: Not specified

FUNNELS
A distinctive feature of the "Tribal"-class destroyers was their two raked funnels, the rearmost of which was later reduced in size to provide a better arc of fire for the ship's AA guns.

MACHINERY
The "Tribal"-class destroyers were powered by two sets of Parsons geared turbines, producing 44,000 shp (33,131 kW) and giving a maximum speed of 36 knots.

STEM
The "Tribal"-class destroyers were quite different from previous designs, featuring a sharply raked stem. This added 10 ft (3 m) to the length of the forecastle deck.

FIRE CONTROL
The "Tribal" class introduced the Fuze Keeping Clock High Angle Fire Control Computer, which was fitted in all subsequent classes of Royal Navy destroyers during World War II.

During her operations in 1939–41, *Cossack* was commanded by Captain Philip Vian, who reached high rank in the Royal Navy and eventually became commander-in-chief of the Home Fleet in the years just after the war.

RIVAL: *FUBUKI*

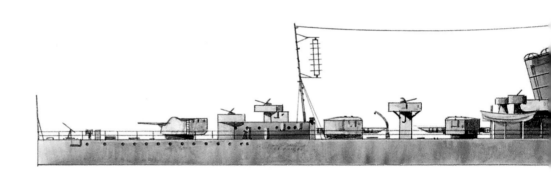

SISTER SHIP: *ESKIMO*

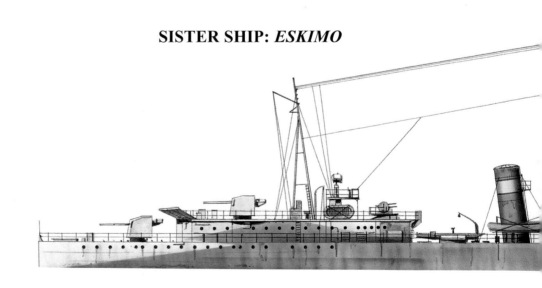

"TRIBAL" CLASS

Only four of the original 16 "Tribals" remained afloat by the end of 1942. Of *Cossack*'s sister ships, *Afridi* and *Gurkha* were bombed off Norway; *Maori* was bombed at Malta; *Mohawk* was torpedoed by an Italian destroyer off Cape Bon; *Zulu* was bombed at Tobruk; *Bedouin* was torpedoed by Italian aircraft; *Mashona* was bombed southwest of Ireland; *Matabele* was sunk by *U454* in the Barents Sea; *Punjabi* was lost in a collision with the *King George V*; *Sikh* was sunk by shore batteries at Tobruk; *Somali* was torpedoed by *U703* south of Iceland; and *Athabaskan* was torpedoed by the German torpedo boat *T27* off the coast of Normandy.

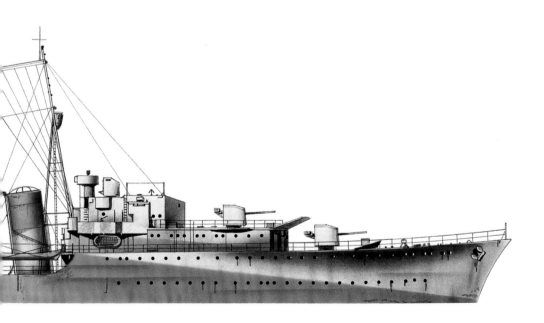

Cossack heads out into the Mediterranean from Malta's Grand Harbor in the summer of 1941. The Royal Navy succeeded in keeping Malta supplied, but only at an enormous cost in ships and men.

***Cossack*'s place in naval history was assured when, in February 1940, she carried out a dramatic rescue operation in Norwegian waters. Taking place during the so-called "Phony War" period, the incident was to generate huge publicity worldwide.**

The use of Norwegian ports by enemy blockade runners was always a sore point. Matters in this respect came to a head when, on February 14, 1940, the tanker *Altmark* (the supply ship of *Admiral Graf Spee*), carrying some 300 merchant seamen from vessels sunk by the pocket battleship, sought refuge in Trondheim under Norwegian protection.

Darkness on February 16 found the enemy tanker in Josing fjord, where she was followed by Captain P.L. Vian in *Cossack*. Vian informed the senior Norwegian officer that as there were British prisoners on the *Altmark*, he demanded the right to search for them. The Norwegian replied that his orders were to resist, and trained his torpedoes on *Cossack*.

Faced with this delicate situation, Vian withdrew and sought the Admiralty's instructions. Three hours later, he was instructed by Winston Churchill, then First Lord of the Admiralty, to board the *Altmark* and liberate the prisoners.

Persuading the Norwegian naval vessels to withdraw, Vian took *Cossack* into Josing fjord and went alongside the *Altmark* – evading an attempt by *Altmark*'s Captain Dau to ram him – and sent over an armed boarding party. Six German guards were killed and six wounded before the boarding party escaped ashore, leaving the British sailors free to break open the *Altmark*'s hatches. Someone asked if there were any British below, and a tremendous yell assured him that the prisoners were all British. The words that followed – "Come on up, then! The Navy's here!"– were to become enshrined in British naval tradition.

DAMAGED AT NARVIK

Only a few weeks later, on April 13, 1940, following the German invasion of Norway, *Cossack* was badly damaged in action with German destroyers at Narvik. Returning to operational duty, she fought a night action near Egersund, attacking a group of ships in German service together with *Ashanti*, *Maori*, and *Sikh* and sinking two of them.

On May 26, 1941, while escorting Convoy WS-8B to the Middle East, *Cossack* and four other destroyers were ordered to break away and head towards the area where the German battleship *Bismarck* had been reported. They found her and made several torpedo attacks in the evening and into the next morning. No hits were scored, but they kept her gunners from getting any sleep, making it more difficult for them to repel other British warships as they attacked her the following morning.

In the summer of 1941 *Cossack* was in Malta on convoy escort duty in the Mediterranean. At this time, she and her sister ship *Maori* shelled the Sardinian harbor of Alghero.

Back in the North Atlantic, she was escorting a convoy from Gibraltar to the United Kingdom on the night of October 23/24, 1941, when she was sighted by the German submarine *U563*, which hit her with a single torpedo.

THE END OF *COSSACK*

On the following day, she was taken in tow by a tug from Gibraltar, but the weather worsened and she sank west of Gibraltar on October 27, 1941, with the loss of 159 crew.

Close-up

Cossack enters harbor in February 1940, where she is greeted by jubilant crowds after rescuing the prisoners of the *Altmark* in Josing fjord.

(1) **Prestige:** The "Tribals" were admired by both their crews and the public, often becoming symbols of prestige while in service.

(2) **Crowds:** It was usual for crowds of dockyard workers and other personnel to gather on the quayside to greet an incoming warship, especially a successful one.

(3) **Armament:** The "Tribals" were built with a plan that differed from other Royal Navy destroyers built up to the time, with more emphasis on guns than torpedoes.

(4) **Technological Innovator:** The "Tribal" class introduced the Fuze Keeping Clock High Angle Fire Control Computer.

(5) **Bow:** The "Tribals" were considered to be handsome ships, with their clipper bow and raked funnels and masts. The bow gave them excellent sea-keeping qualities.

(6) **Corvette:** The "Tribals" were much larger and so different from other British destroyers in service that the resurrection of a corvette classification was considered for them.

Hiryu 1937

The Japanese carrier *Hiryu*, which translates as "Flying Dragon," was so successful a design that it became the standard for the Imperial Japanese Navy. Construction of *Hiryu* was delayed to include some improvements in her seakeeping qualities.

FLIGHT DECK
Hiryu was relatively small for a fleet carrier, which was reflected in the size of her flight deck. The position of the island on the port side proved a failure, as it created dangerous air currents and reduced deck space.

HANGARS
Hiryu's two hangars were served by three lifts. The carrier could accommodate about 70 aircraft, but her usual complement was 54 (18 Mitsubishi A6M Zeros, 18 Aichi D3A Vals, and 18 Nakajima B5N Kates).

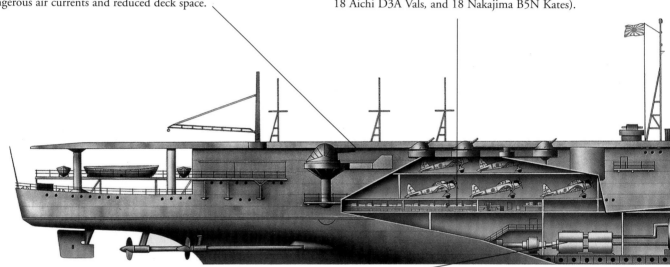

MACHINERY
Hiryu was powered by four Kanpon geared turbines, producing 153,000 shp (113 MW) and giving a speed of just over 34 knots. Oil capacity was 4,400 tons (3,992 tonnes) and endurance was 10,330 nm (19,131 km) at 18 knots.

HIRYU – SPECIFICATION

Country of origin: Japan
Type: Aircraft carrier
Laid down: July 8, 1936
Launched: November 16, 1937
Commissioned: July 5, 1939
Decommissioned: n/a
Fate: Sunk June 5, 1942, Battle of Midway
Complement: 1,103 + 23 officers for Carrier Division 2 Flagship

Dimensions:
Displacement: (standard) 17,300 tons (15,694 tonnes); (full load) 20,165 tons (18,293 tonnes)
Length: (waterline) 728 ft 5 in (222 m); 711 ft 7 in (216.9 m) (flight deck)
Beam: 73 ft 2 in (22.3 m)

Draught: 25 ft 5 in (7.74 m)

Power plant:
Propulsion: 4 shaft geared steam turbines producing 153,000 shp (113 MW)
Speed: 63.9 km/hs (34.5 knots)
Range: 10,330 nm (19,131 km) at 18 knots

Armament & Armor:
Armament: 12 x 5-in (127-mm) guns; 31x 0.98-in (25-mm) anti-aircraft guns
Armor: Not specified
Aircraft: 70

F A C T S

- Launched November 16, 1937; completed July 1939.

- Took part in the attack on Pearl Harbor, December 7, 1941.

- Air strikes against Wake Island, December 21–23, 1941.

- Air strikes on Darwin, February 1942.

- Raid on Ceylon, April 1942.

- Severely damaged by U.S. aircraft in Battle of Midway, June 4, 1942, and sunk by escorting destroyers the following day (416 dead).

SUPERSTRUCTURE
The island was situated almost amidships and to port, where it partly balanced the two horizontally discharging funnels to starboard. The only other Japanese carrier to share this feature was *Akagi*.

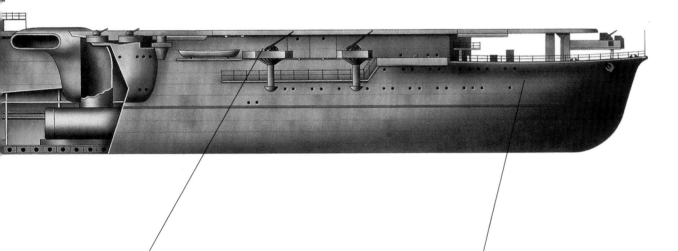

ARMAMENT
Both *Hiryu* and her sister ship *Soryu*, which translates as "Blue Dragon," carried a main armament of 12 5-in (127-mm) dual-purpose guns and 31 0.98-in (25-mm) anti-aircraft guns.

HULL
The *Hiryu* was a slightly enlarged and modified *Soryu*, with the beam increased by 3 ft (1 m) to give a 20 percent increase in oil capacity. Her protection was also strengthened and her forecastle was raised by a deck.

Naval air power was at the core of Japan's
strategy. She had completed her first aircraft
carrier, the *Hosho*, in 1922, and this vessel was
soon to be followed by larger and more powerful
fleet carriers, like the *Akagi*, seen here.

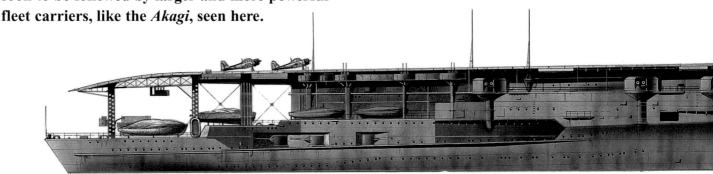

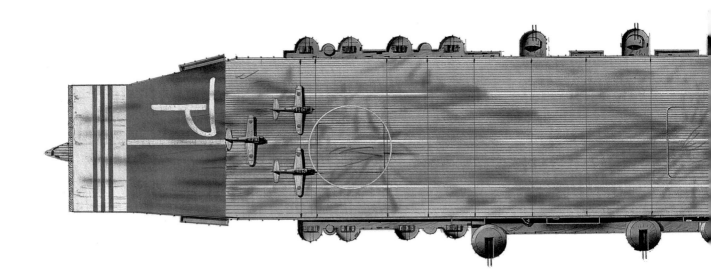

FAST-ATTACK CARRIERS

At the outset of the Pacific War in December 1941, Japan possessed the third-largest fleet in the world, with fast-attack carriers manned by highly trained crews at its core. The navy, however, had certain deficiencies that were to prove fatal. Few anti-submarine warships had been built, merchant shipping was not protected by a convoy system, and radar was not advanced enough for operational use. Moreover, the Japanese did not have the raw material resources necessary to wage a major war for any length of time. They therefore relied on rapid conquest, preceded by the neutralization of enemy assets by means of their fast-attack carriers.

JAPANESE CARRIER: *AKAGI*

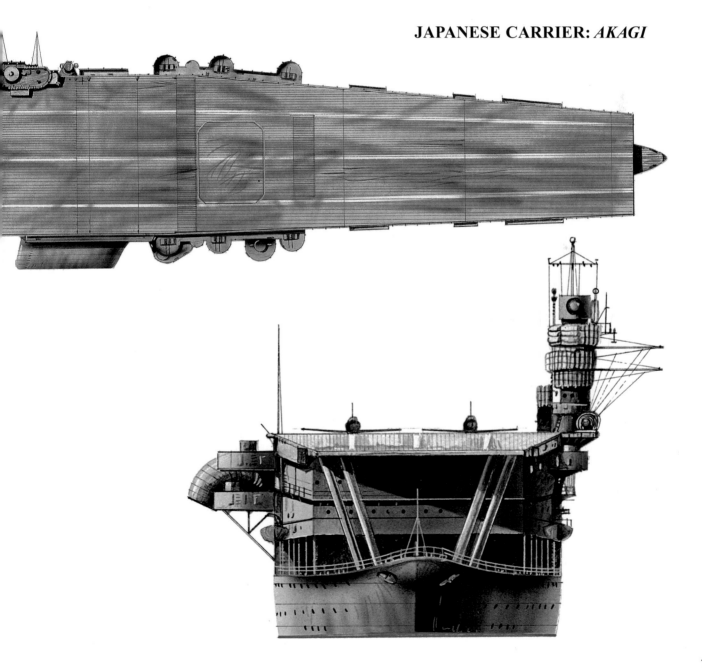

In November 1941, *Hiryu* formed part of the most formidable force assembled in Japanese waters since Tsushima, 36 years earlier. This was the battle fleet assigned by the Imperial Japanese Navy to what was known as the Hawaiian Operation, the planned surprise attack on Pearl Harbor, the principal base of the U.S. Pacific Fleet.

The Japanese Fleet sailed for Hawaii on November 26, 1941. At its heart were the aircraft carriers of the 1st Air Fleet, the *Akagi*, *Kaga*, *Hiryu*, *Soryu*, *Zuikaku*, and *Shokaku*, under the command of Vice-Admiral Chuichi Nagumo.

The first attack on Pearl Harbor lasted 30 minutes, striking the anchorage and outlying air bases. The second

Close-up

Hiryu met her end in the open ocean, but other carriers, like the *Aso*, seen here, were scuttled or bombed to destruction in harbor.

(1) **Bridge:** The design of the *Amagi*-class carriers, of which *Aso* was one, closely followed that of the *Hiryu*, but with the bridge on the starboard side.

(2) **Power:** Due to a lack of suitable engines, *Aso* was powered by destroyer turbines. Other ships in the class used cruiser turbines.

(3) **Incomplete:** Work on *Aso* was stopped in January 1945 when she was 60 percent complete. She was launched and left in an unfinished state.

(4) **Three completed:** Laid down in 1942–43, only three carriers of this class were completed. Others were in various stages of completion.

(5) **Hull:** This was used as a kamikaze testbed and she was half-sunk in shallow water at Kure when surrendered in August 1945.

(6) **Filling the gap:** *Aso* was one of the carriers laid down to fill the gap left by the destruction of Japan's fleet carriers at Midway, but work began too late.

Shinano *was the most modern of Japan's carriers. Adapted from a* Yamato-*class battleship, she was sunk by the American submarine* Archerfish *on November 29, 1944, while en route from Yokosuka to another naval yard for fitting out.*

strike, just over an hour later, was made by 54 Kate bombers, 78 Val dive-bombers and 35 fighters. The strike lasted 65 minutes but was hampered by dense smoke from the burning anchorage and by heavy anti-aircraft fire, as well as by small numbers of American fighters. Of the 94 warships in the harbor, 18 were sunk or suffered major damage. Eight of the losses were battleships, which had been the attackers' primary targets.

After the Pearl Harbor attack, *Hiryu* was assigned to Carrier Division 2. She participated in the launching of air strikes against Wake Island, and in January 1942 she supported the invasion of Ambon in the Moluccas. In February 1942, together with *Soryu*, she launched air attacks on Darwin, Australia, and in March she took part in the Battle of the Java Sea, her aircraft attacking Allied shipping and sinking a Dutch freighter.

ATTACKS ON CEYLON AND COLOMBO

In April 1942, Admiral Nagumo's 1st Carrier Striking Force, comprising the aircraft carriers *Akagi*, *Hiryu*, *Shokaku*, *Soryu*, and *Zuikaku*, entered the Indian Ocean to carry out an attack on Ceylon. Between them, the five carriers mustered some 300 strike aircraft and fighters.

Early on April 5 (Easter Sunday) the Japanese launched a strike of 53 Nakajima B5N Kate high-level bombers and 38 Aichi D3A Val dive-bombers, escorted by 36 Zero fighters, to attack Colombo. The Japanese raiding force was intercepted by 42 Hurricanes and Fulmars, resulting in fierce air battles developing over the city and harbor. In

the end, seven Japanese aircraft were destroyed, but 19 British fighters were shot down. The attack caused heavy damage to built-up areas. The damage to shipping and the port installations was relatively light, although the auxiliary cruiser *Hector* and the destroyer *Tenedos* were sunk.

At about noon, the cruisers *Cornwall* and *Dorsetshire* were sighted by a reconnaissance aircraft from the heavy cruiser *Tone* and 53 Val dive-bombers were immediately sent out to attack them. The bombing was devastatingly accurate and both ships were sunk.

THE TIDE OF WAR TURNS

At the beginning of June 1942, the Japanese launched a strong thrust in the central Pacific; its objective, as part of Yamamoto's eastward expansion plan, was to occupy Midway Island. The thrust was led by a four-carrier Mobile Force comprising the *Akagi*, *Kaga*, *Hiryu* and *Soryu*, supported by heavy units of the First Fleet and covered by a diversionary attack by carrier aircraft on Dutch Harbor in the Aleutians.

In the ensuing battle, which effectively turned the tide of the Pacific War, the U.S. Navy destroyed all four fleet carriers, three-quarters of the Imperial Japanese Navy's carrier striking force, for the loss of 94 aircraft and the carrier *Yorktown*. On June 4, *Hiryu* was crippled in an attack by 24 Douglas SBD dive-bombers from *Enterprise*. Her burnt-out hulk was sunk by a Japanese destroyer the next day.

Bismarck 1939

The mighty battleship *Bismarck* was to have formed the nucleus of a powerful battle group that included the battlecruisers *Scharnhorst* and *Gneisenau* and the heavy cruiser *Prinz Eugen*. *Bismarck* was capable of engaging escorting warships single-handedly while her consorts attacked the merchant convoys.

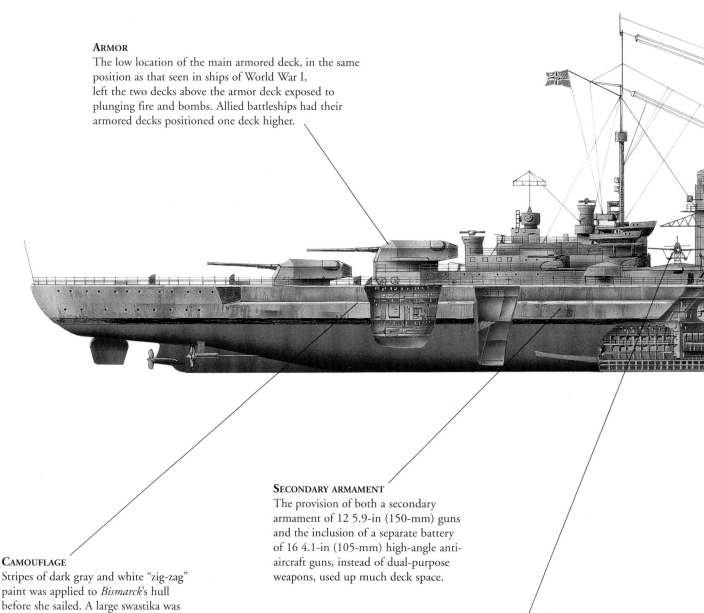

ARMOR
The low location of the main armored deck, in the same position as that seen in ships of World War I, left the two decks above the armor deck exposed to plunging fire and bombs. Allied battleships had their armored decks positioned one deck higher.

CAMOUFLAGE
Stripes of dark gray and white "zig-zag" paint was applied to *Bismarck*'s hull before she sailed. A large swastika was superimposed on a gray band of paint, applied across the breadth of the deck near the bow, for identification purposes.

SECONDARY ARMAMENT
The provision of both a secondary armament of 12 5.9-in (150-mm) guns and the inclusion of a separate battery of 16 4.1-in (105-mm) high-angle anti-aircraft guns, instead of dual-purpose weapons, used up much deck space.

AIRCRAFT
An aircraft catapult was fitted amidships and provision was made for the battleship to carry six Arado Ar 196 seaplanes, although *Bismarck* carried only four. These were fast enough and sufficiently armed to intercept Allied maritime reconnaissance aircraft.

RADAR

Bismarck carried Seetakt radar. Maximum range against a ship-sized target at sea was up to 136 miles (220 km) in favorable conditions, though more typically half that.

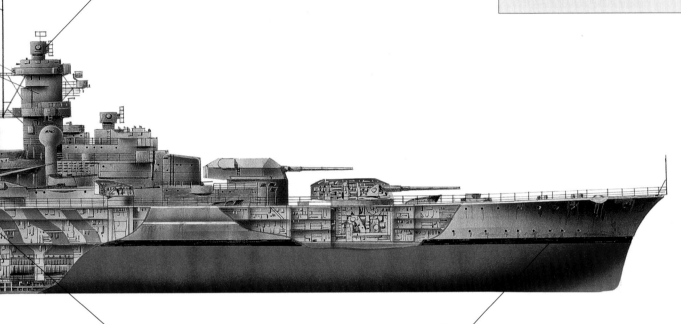

TORPEDO TUBES

Bismarck was fitted with eight 21-in (533-mm) torpedo tubes, four on either side of the main deck amidships.

BOW

Both *Bismarck* and *Tirpitz* were designed with a straight bow, but this was changed to a rakish clipper bow after launching.

BISMARCK – SPECIFICATION

Country of origin: Germany
Type: Battleship
Laid down: July 1, 1936
Builder: Blohm & Voss, Hamburg
Launched: February 14, 1939
Commissioned: August 24, 1940
Fate: Sunk May 27, 1941
Complement: 2,092: 103 officers 1,989 men (1941)

Dimensions:
Displacement: (standard) 51,809 tons (47,000 tonnes); (full load) 56,108 tons (50,900 tonnes)
Length: (overall) 823.5 ft (251 m); (waterline) 792.3 ft (241.5 m)
Beam: 118.1 ft (36 m) (waterline)

Draught: (Standard) 30.5 ft (9.3 m); (full load) 33.5 ft (10.2 m)

Power plant:
Propulsion: 3 Blohm & Voss geared turbines 150,170 shp (111.98 MW)
Speed: 31.1 knots
Range: 8,525 nm (15,788 km)

Armament & Armor:
Armament: 8 x 15-in (380-mm) guns; 12 x 5.9-in (150-mm) guns; 16 x 4.1-in (105-mm anti-aircraft guns)
Armor: 4.3–14 in (110–360 mm)
Aircraft: 4 x Arado Ar 196 A-3, with 1 double-ended catapult

Bismarck and Tirpitz were to have been followed by a
class of even more powerful battleships. Six units
were planned, and the first two were laid down, but
the project was abandoned in the middle of 1940
when Germany seemed to be winning the war.

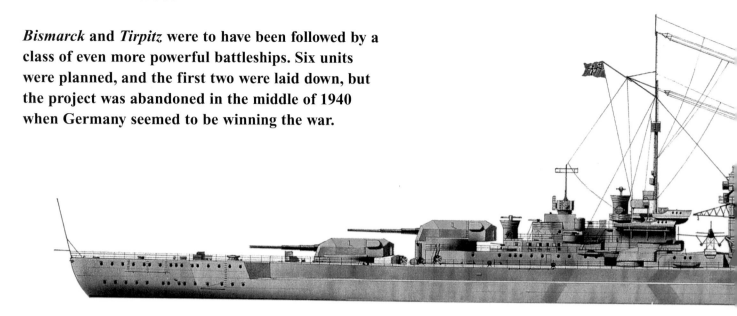

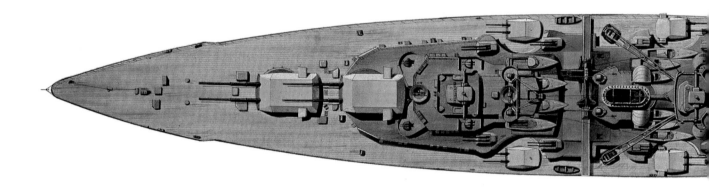

BISMARCK

DEPLOYMENT TO THE ATLANTIC

On April 2, 1941, the German Naval Staff issued preparatory orders for the deployment of *Bismarck* and other surface units to the Atlantic. In the next New Moon period at the end of the month *Bismarck*, *Prinz Eugen*, and the battlecruiser *Gneisenau*, which was then in the French Atlantic port of Brest together with her sister ship, *Scharnhorst*, were to rendezvous in the Atlantic to launch a combined attack on Allied shipping. Had this formidable battle group put to sea in its entirety, the result might have been disastrous for Britain. The carnage this group was capable of inflicting, as the British were well aware, would have been atrocious.

"Ship no longer maneuverable. We fight to the last shell. Long live the Führer." With these words, Admiral Günther Lütjens, the German Fleet Commander, signalled *Bismarck*'s impending doom to Berlin.

Bismarck had sailed only days earlier, on May 19, 1941, in company with *Prinz Eugen*. There was to be no rendezvous. *Scharnhorst* was laid up with boiler trouble and *Gneisenau* had been torpedoed in Brest harbor by a Bristol Beaufort of RAF Coastal Command on April 6.

Air reconnaissance revealed that the German warships were heading for Icelandic waters, and the Royal Navy rapidly deployed its forces to intercept them. On May 23 they were sighted by the cruisers *Suffolk* and *Norfolk*, which continued to shadow the ships at high speed throughout the night, *Suffolk* maintaining contact with her Type 284 radar.

Close-up

After her launch, *Bismarck* was towed to the equipping pier to be fitted out. Even though the hull was completed and the machinery was installed, months of work lay ahead before she was finished.

1. **Armament:** The secondary armament of 12 5.9-in (150-mm) guns were installed in twin turrets, three to port and three to starboard.

2. **Aircraft hangar:** The large aircraft hangar was situated amidships aft of the funnel and housing up to six Arado Ar 196 floatplanes.

3. **Seetakt radar:** Used for navigation and search purposes, this has yet to be fitted on top of the bridge.

4. **Rangefinder:** Other equipment to be fitted includes the rangefinder, which will be installed in a cupola on the conning tower.

5. **Mast:** The mainmast is taking shape to the rear of the funnel, with its spotting positions and signalling equipment.

6. **Searchlight:** The ship was fitted with a very powerful searchlight, which was covered when not in use. The cover is seen here in the lowered position.

Huge crowds attended the launch of Bismarck *on February 14, 1939. The ceremony was carried out by Dorothea von Löwenfeld, Bismarck's granddaughter. Adolf Hitler, Hermann Göring, and Rudolf Hess were among those in attendance.*

GERMAN SHIPS DESTROY *HOOD*

The British battleship *Prince of Wales* and the battlecruiser *Hood*, meanwhile, were coming up quickly. At 0537 the opposing forces sighted each other at a range of 17 miles (27 km), and opened fire at 0553. Both German ships concentrated their fire on *Hood* and, thanks to their stereoscopic rangefinders, straddled her immediately. *Bismarck*'s second and third salvoes struck the battlecruiser amidships, and those from *Prinz Eugen* started a fire among her ready-to-use AA ammunition. At 0600, as the British warships were altering course in order to bring all their guns to bear, *Hood* was hit again by a salvo, which pierced her lightly armored decks and detonated in her after magazines. She blew up with a tremendous explosion and disappeared with a speed that stunned all who witnessed the event. Only three of her crew of 1,419 officers and seamen survived.

As *Prince of Wales* altered course sharply to avoid the wreckage she herself came under heavy fire. Within moments she sustained hits by four 15-in (380-mm) and three 8-in (203-mm) shells, one of which exploded on the bridge and killed or wounded almost everyone there except her captain, who ordered the battleship to turn away under cover of smoke. *Prince of Wales*'s gunners had obtained

three hits on *Bismarck*, causing two of her fuel tanks to leak oil and contaminating others. Because of this, Admiral Lütjens decided to abandon the sortie and to steer southwest for St. Nazaire, the only port on the Atlantic coast of France with a dry dock large enough to accommodate his flagship while repairs were carried out. He detached *Prinz Eugen* to continue on her way alone.

HUNTERS CLOSE IN

The main concern now was to reduce *Bismarck*'s speed, giving the hunters a chance to close in for the kill. At 1440 on May 24 the British commander, Admiral Tovey, ordered the carrier *Victorious* to race ahead to a flying-off point 100 miles (160 km) from the enemy ships and launch a strike against them. The first strike by Swordfish aircraft resulted in only one torpedo hit, but the second was decisive. Two torpedoes found their mark. One struck *Bismarck*'s extreme stern, damaging her propellers and jamming her rudders.

The British warships closed in during the night to finish her off. By 1020 *Bismarck* had been reduced to a blazing wreck, with all her armament out of action, but she was still afloat and it was left to the cruisers *Norfolk* and *Dorsetshire* to close in and sink her with torpedoes.

Iowa 1942

Although the U.S. Navy laid much emphasis on the construction of aircraft carriers between the wars, they did not neglect battleships. In the late 1930s three new classes of fast battleship emerged: *North Carolina* of 1937; *South Dakota* of 1938; and the *Iowa*-class of 1939. The basis was being laid for the task forces that would one day dominate the Pacific.

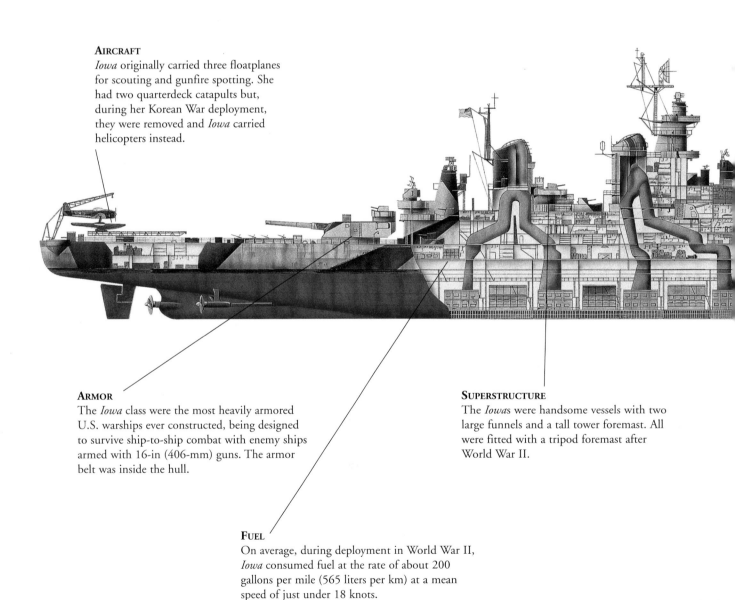

AIRCRAFT
Iowa originally carried three floatplanes for scouting and gunfire spotting. She had two quarterdeck catapults but, during her Korean War deployment, they were removed and *Iowa* carried helicopters instead.

ARMOR
The *Iowa* class were the most heavily armored U.S. warships ever constructed, being designed to survive ship-to-ship combat with enemy ships armed with 16-in (406-mm) guns. The armor belt was inside the hull.

SUPERSTRUCTURE
The *Iowa*s were handsome vessels with two large funnels and a tall tower foremast. All were fitted with a tripod foremast after World War II.

FUEL
On average, during deployment in World War II, *Iowa* consumed fuel at the rate of about 200 gallons per mile (565 liters per km) at a mean speed of just under 18 knots.

DESIGN
Iowa's design included a clipper bow and long foredeck, with graceful sheer. They were the fastest battleships ever built, with a high length-to-beam ratio.

ARMAMENT
The Mk VII 16-in (406-mm) main armament fired projectiles weighing up to 2,700 lbg (1,225 kg) over a maximum distance of 23 miles (39 km).

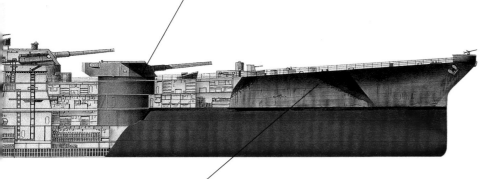

FACTS

- Launched August 27, 1942; completed February 1943.

- Damaged by grounding off Maine, July 16, 1943.

- Carried President Roosevelt to Casablanca Conference, October 1943.

- Bombardments of Luzon and Formosa, Leyte, and Okinawa, 1944–45.

- Refit 1951.

- Recommissioned for service in Korean War, 1952.

- Atlantic Fleet, 1952–58.

- Decommissioned 1958.

- Reactivated 1984.

- Gun turret wrecked by explosion, 1989; 47 dead.

- Decommissioned 1990.

MACHINERY
Iowa was powered by four General Electric geared turbines, producing 212,000 shp (158.09 MW). The design maximum speed was 33 knots, but all the *Iowa*-class ships reached 35 knots in service.

IOWA – SPECIFICATION

Country of origin: USA
Type: Battleship
Laid down: June 27, 1940
Builder: New York Naval Yard
Launched: August 27, 1942
Commissioned: February 22, 1943
Decommissioned: October 26, 1990
Fate: Struck March 17, 2006
Complement: 151 officers, 2,637 enlisted

Dimensions:
Displacement: 45,000 tons (40,823 tonnes)
Length: 887 ft 3 in (270.43 m)
Beam: 108 ft 2 in (32.9 m)
Draught: 37 ft 2 in (11.33 m)

Power plant:
Propulsion: Quadruple screw turbines delivering 212,000 shp (1,58.09 MW)
Speed: 33 knots
Range: 15,000 nm (27,780 km) @ 12 knots

Armament & Armor:
Armament: 9 x 16-in (406-mm) guns; 20 x 5-in (127-mm) guns
Armor:
  Belt: 12.1 in (307.3 mm)
  Turrets: 19.7 in (500 mm)
  Decks: 7.5 in (190.50 mm)
Aircraft: Floatplanes and helicopters

Designs for the *Iowa* class of battleship were
started in 1936 in response to reports that the
Japanese were laying down battleships of 46,000
tons (41,730 tonnes). *Iowa* was laid down in 1940
and commissioned in 1943.

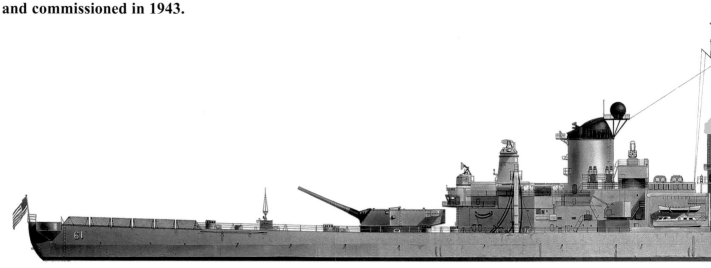

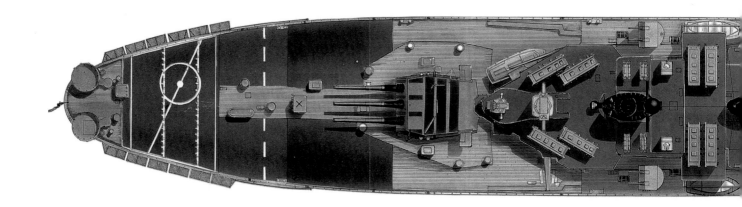

IOWA (POST-WAR REFIT)

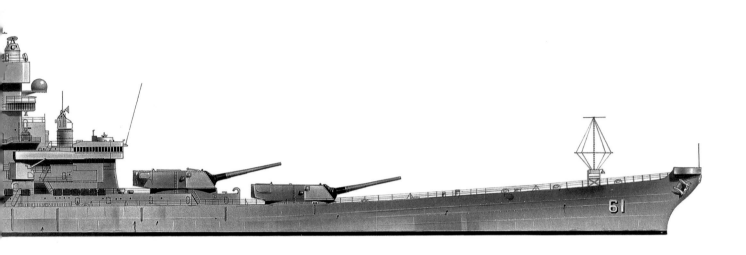

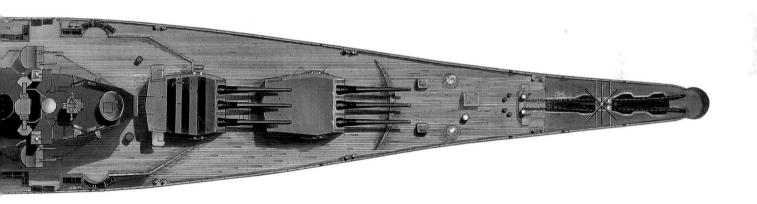

IOWA CLASS

The *Iowa* class, which included the *Missouri*, *New Jersey*, and *Wisconsin*, had a greater displacement than the previous *South Dakota* class, and had more power and protection. They served mainly as escorts for carrier task groups during World War II, being the only battleships fast enough to keep up with them. *Iowa* was recommissioned for service in the Korean War, being used to bombard shore targets in North Korea. Two more *Iowa*-class ships were laid down; the *Illinois* was cancelled when construction was 22 percent complete, and *Kentucky* was launched in 1950 to clear the slip while still incomplete. Her bow section was subsequently used to repair damage to the *Wisconsin*.

The *Iowa*-class battleships were the largest and fastest battleships ever constructed for the U.S. Navy. They were also the last.

Iowa's designers set out to create the finest battleship possible. The fact that all the *Iowa*s that were commissioned were still on active service half a century later bears witness to their success. The ships had to be able to pass through the Panama

Close-up

The role of the new fast battleships like *Iowa* was not merely to ward off possible surface attacks on the all-important aircraft carriers, but also to provide additional anti-aircraft firepower.

(1) **Armament:** The *Iowa* firing her 16-in (406-mm) guns in a broadside. Her main turrets were protected by 9.5-17 in (241–432 mm) of armor plating.

(2) **Armor:** The *Iowa* class carried the same armament as earlier U.S. battleships, but their length was increased because of the increased armor protection.

(3) **Length to beam:** These were the fastest battleships ever built, with a high length-to-beam ratio.

(4) **Mast:** All the *Iowa* class were fitted with a high tripod mainmast after World War II and their aircraft catapults were removed.

(5) **Electronics:** After *Iowa* was reactivated in 1983, it was found that the shock of firing her main armament caused problems with newly installed electronic equipment.

(6) **Designation:** *Iowa* was the fourth battleship in the U.S. Navy to be named in honor of the 29th state, and the last lead ship of any class of U.S. battleships.

Iowa's sleek lines are easy to see in this photograph, which reveals her long, narrow bow section to good advantage. The Iowa*s were arguably the most aesthetically pleasing of the modern battleships.*

Canal, which meant that the beam could be no wider than 116 ft (33.55 m). The *Iowa*s displaced close to 60,000 tons (54,431 tonnes) at extra-deep load, yet they were still capable of making well over 30 knots. Such impressive performance was possible because she had 60 percent more power and the fact that she was longer by almost 30 percent than the preceding *South Dakota* class.

The long, narrow bow in particular, with its considerable sheer, was an outstanding feature of the *Iowa*s. They had the same protection as the earlier class and the same main armament, but the barrels were lengthened by five calibers. This development increased their effective range to a maximum of 21 nm (38.8 km) for a shell that weighed about the same as a small car. The battleships also carried enormous numbers of light AA guns, though most of these were removed at the end of World War II.

Iowa was built at the New York Naval Yard and commissioned on February 22, 1943. She operated out of Atlantic ports for almost a year, her operational career being interrupted briefly when she ran aground off Maine in July 1943, and then deployed to the Pacific, where she spent the rest of the war. During the Battle of Leyte Gulf, on October 25, 1944, Task Force 34 was formed from the battleships *Iowa, New Jersey, Washington, Alabama,* *Massachusetts,* and *Indiana,* four cruisers and 10 destroyers, with the intent to eradicate a Japanese diversionary force, approaching from the north under Vice-Admiral Ozawa. Instead, Admiral Halsey, flying his flag on *New Jersey,* took his ships south to hunt down what remained of the main enemy force, leaving carrier aircraft to deal with Ozawa. This tactic succeeded, and the carriers *Chitose, Zuikaku, Zuiho,* and *Chiyoda,* as well as a destroyer, were all sunk.

RETURN TO THE ATLANTIC

In 1953, after Korean War service, she returned to the Atlantic. On one occasion, together with *Wisconsin,* she exercised with Britain's last battleship, *Vanguard,* the last time an Anglo-American battleship force went to sea together.

Iowa was reactivated twice, first in 1951–58 and then in 1983–90. She received new fire control and multi-functional radar systems, Tomahawk and Harpoon cruise missiles, and upgraded communications equipment. In 1989, an explosion in one of *Iowa*'s 16-in (406-mm) gun turrets killed 47 officers and men; plans for repairs were deferred when it was decided that *Iowa* and *New Jersey* would be mothballed in 1991. In fact, *Iowa* was paid off in October 1990 and *New Jersey* in February 1991. In 2009, *Iowa* was waiting to be officially allocated as a museum ship in Vallejo, California.

TYPE XXI U-BOAT

The Type XXI U-Boat was a milestone in the development of the submarine, and a significant step forward on the evolutionary road that led to the nuclear-powered vessels of today. In all, 121 units were commissioned, but relatively few became operational.

MACHINERY
The Type XXI class was powered by two-shaft diesel/electric motors. It was the first submarine to be faster underwater than on the surface. It also had creeping electric motors designed for silent running.

HULL
The Type XXI class had a distinctive streamlined double-pressure hull and a low faired-in conning tower.

BATTERY COMPARTMENT
The battery compartment was more sophisticated than found in other classes. It had three 124-cell batteries for 33,900 ampere/hours, which was some three times the capacity of the earlier Type XXI class.

SNORKEL
The Type XXI was fitted with a *schnorkel* (snorkel), a simple pipe with a valve on one end, which extended above sea level while the boat was submerged. The device enabled the U-boat to run on diesel engines even when underwater.

ARMAMENT
Although Type XXI had provision for four 1.18-in (30-mm) guns in twin mountings, four 0.79-in (20-mm) guns were usually carried.

TORPEDOES
The Type XXI class was fitted with six 21-in (533-mm) torpedo tubes, with storage for 23 torpedoes or 14 torpedoes plus 12 mines. The torpedoes were self-loading.

TYPE XXI – SPECIFICATION

Country of origin: Germany
Type: Submarine
In production: 1943–45
Builder: Blohm & Voss, Hamburg; AG Weser, Bremen; F. Schichau, Danzig
Launched: April 19, 1944
Fate: N/A
Complement: 57

Dimensions:
Displacement: (standard) 1,787 tons (1,621 tonnes): (full load) 2,315 tons (2,100 tonnes)
Length: 251 ft 8 in (76.7 m); **Beam:** 26 ft 3 in (8 m); **Draught:** 17 ft 5 in (5.3 m)

Power plant:
Propulsion: 2 x supercharged 6-cylinder diesel engines delivering 4,000 shp (2.9 MW); 2 x double-acting electric motors delivering 4,959 shp (3.7 MW); 2 x silent-running electric motors delivering 222.5 shp (166 kW)
Speed (surfaced): 15.9 knots (diesel); 17.9 knots (electric)
Speed (submerged): 17.2 knots (electric); 6.1 knots (silent-running motors)
Range (surfaced): 15,500 nm (28,706 km) at 10 knots
Range (submerged): 340 nm (630 km) at 5 knots

Armament & Armor:
Armament: 4 x 0.79-in (20-mm) cannon; 6 x 21-in (533-mm) torpedo tubes (23 torpedoes)

The ocean-going U-boat proved a fearsome weapon
in World War II, and one that came close to bringing
Britain to her knees in the bitter conflict known as
the Battle of the Atlantic. Had the Type XXIs been
available earlier in numbers, they might have
massacred the Allied Atlantic convoys.

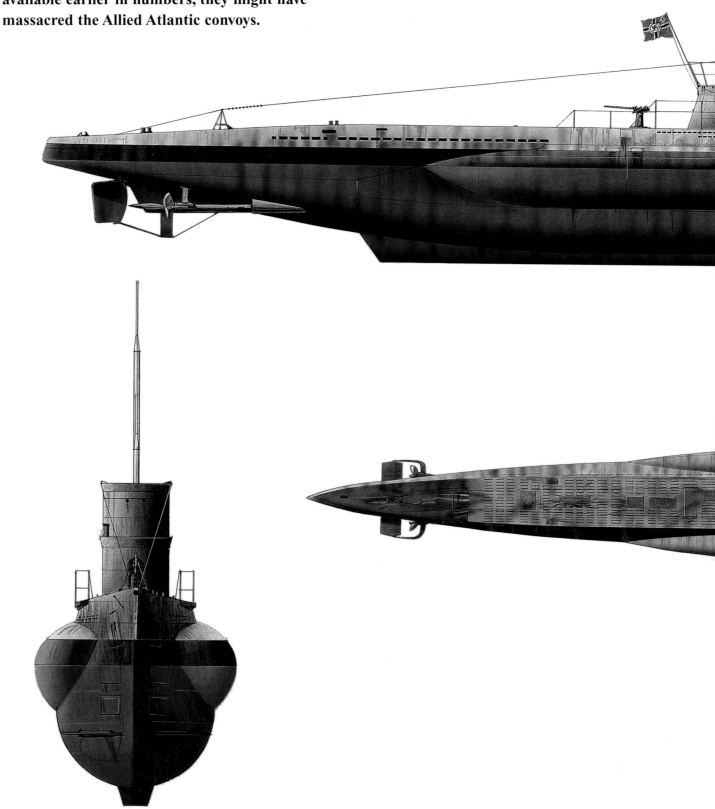

TYPE VII U BOAT: U47

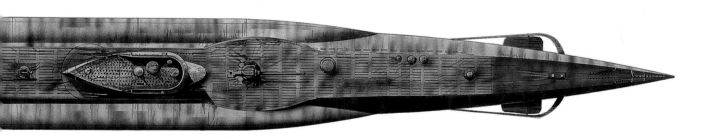

TYPES XXI AND XXIII

In the latter months of the war Germany launched a massive submarine construction program, the aim of which was to get two types of submarine – the Type XXI and the Type XXIII – into service as quickly as possible. By the end of the war 55 Type XXIs were operational and 57 Type XXIIIs were either at sea, in various stages of construction, or projected. The building program was severely disrupted by Allied bombing. This was fortunate for the Allies because both boats were utterly lethal war machines.

With the Battle of the Atlantic being won by the Allies, the requirement for building the Type XXI was so urgent that Germany decided to begin series production before a prototype had even been tested. They also decided to build the boat in sections.

Because no testing had taken place, the first six Type XXIs proved to be unfit for operational service and were relegated to training duties. Three types of shipyard were engaged in the work of construction. The first built the sections of pressure and external hulls and bulkheads, the plating and frames having been received already cut and set to shape by the steelmakers. Some 32 shipyards and structural engineering firms were engaged in this stage, and a massive dispersal program had to be implemented because of Allied bombing. The sections were then transported to 16 other firms, usually by water, and all the wiring, pipework and main and auxiliary engines were installed. Finally, the sections were welded together in three building yards and the completed vessel was subjected to testing.

Although the first Type XXI U-Boat, *U2501*, was launched in May 1944, she was one of the boats found to be defective and the type did not become operational until

Close-up

The Type XXIs were ocean-going boats capable of fully submerged operations using the *schnorkel* and conventional diesel/electric drive. Their hulls were streamlined.

(1) Design: Prior to 1943 U-boats were constructed on conventional lines. Some 16 firms were involved, using designs prepared by the German Admiralty.

(2) Prefabrication: In 1943, a program of dispersal and prefabrication was set up because of the increase in bombing and to make better use of resources.

(3) Hull: 32 German shipyards were made responsible for the fabrication of pressure and external hulls, as well as bulkheads.

(4) Transport: The sections were sent, usually by water, to 16 other firms for installation of all wiring, pipework and engines.

(5) Welding: The various sections were then welded together by three building yards, which carried out initial trials before handing the U-boats over to the navy.

(6) Hull: In the Type XXI, surface sea-keeping qualities and gun armament were sacrificed to give a streamlined hull for higher submerged speed.

This photograph shows a Type XXI being launched. The first six Type XXIs were unfit for operational use. Some of the factories producing the plating and frames had worked to excessive tolerances, so the six examples they built were relegated to training duties.

March 1945, with the *U2511*. Although 740 Type XXIs were ordered, only 21 were completed, and of the 55 commissioned, only two made operational sorties. The first operational boat, *U2511*, deployed to the Norwegian port of Bergen and set out on her first and only war patrol early in May. On the 4th, she sighted a British cruiser, but her captain, having been advised that the German surrender was imminent, elected to set up only a dummy attack on the warship, so saving its crew and probably his own.

SUPER-LIGHT BATTERIES

The Type XXI was a double-hulled vessel, with a high submerged speed and the ability to run silently at 3.5 knots thanks to her electric "creeper" motors. The outer hull was constructed of light plating to aid streamlining, while the inner hull was reinforced with 1.1–1.45 in (28–37 mm) of thick carbon steel plating. With her new, super-light batteries, she could maintain a submerged speed of 16 knots for one hour; at four knots, she could remain submerged for three days on a single charge.

The Type XXIs were eagerly seized by the Allies at the end of the war. The *U2518*, surrendered to Britain, went to France in 1947 and was extensively tested as the *Roland Morillot*, forming the basis for the French Navy's *Narval* class of five boats laid down between 1951 and 1956. Their long range enabled them to make a fast transit to France's overseas colonies, followed by a patrol of seven to 14 days. Another boat, the *U2540*, was salvaged and recommissioned by the West German Bundesmarine as the *Wilhelm Bauer*.

ONE TYPE XXI SURVIVING

The Soviet Union's first post-war submarine, the "Whiskey" class, was essentially a modified version of the Type XXI. The Russians went on to mass-produce 236 submarines between 1949 and 1957.

The first Type XXI, *U2501*, spent her operational career on training duties in the Baltic. On May 3, 1945, she was scuttled by her crew in Hamburg. Only six Type XXIs survived the war intact. One was salvaged and is today preserved as a museum exhibit in Bremerhaven.

Modern Ships 1950–Present

During the early years of the Cold War era, it was apparent that the aircraft carrier, like the battleship before it, was becoming increasingly vulnerable to attack from the air and under the sea, and it needed powerful defensive measures to support it.

The Sovremenny-*class destroyers were designed to engage hostile ships by means of missile attack, and to provide warships and transport ships with protection against ship and air attack.*

In the 1950s, the Americans and Russians both began to explore the concept of the nuclear-powered ballistic missile submarine, a vessel capable of remaining submerged for lengthy periods, making use of the polar ice-cap and various oceanic features to remain undetected. Armed with nuclear-tipped rockets, it would be the ultimate deterrent. The world's first nuclear-powered submarine was the American *Nautilus*, launched on January 21, 1954.

FIRST NUCLEAR SUBMARINE

Although the Americans were the first to make the nuclear-powered submarine breakthrough, with an early class of boat based on the prototype *Nautilus*, what the U.S. Navy really wanted was to merge the new technologies of ballistic missiles, smaller thermonuclear weapons, and inertial guidance systems into a single weapon system. They succeeded with the deployment, in 1960, of the first Fleet Ballistic Missile (FBM) submarine, armed with the Polaris A1 missile. The Russians' first nuclear submarine design was the "November" class, which was designed for the anti-ship rather than the anti-submarine role. Armed with nuclear torpedoes, the task of these boats was to attack carrier battle groups. They were very noisy underwater and were prone to reactor leaks, which did not endear them to their crews. They were involved in numerous accidents. The inability of the USSR to match the United

States in terms of sea power was apparent in October 1962, when the Americans imposed a blockade of Cuba following the infiltration of Soviet strategic and tactical missiles, as well as Il-28 jet bombers, into the island. Lacking the means to break the quarantine, and unwilling to risk all-out nuclear war, Premier Khrushchev was compelled to back down and order the removal of the missiles and bombers.

MISSILE-CARRYING WEAPONS

The Cuban Crisis taught the Russians a stern lesson in the importance of sea power, and future Soviet naval policies were amended accordingly. A pattern of bi-annual exercises was established in 1963; in March and April seven surface units plus support vessels exercised near the Lofotens, and in

The USS Nimitz *and her sister ships form the nucleus of a U.S. fleet's Battle Force, the principal task force in the U.S. Navy.* Nimitz *forms part of Carrier Strike Group 11.*

August a similar force conducted exercises in the Iceland-Faeroes Gap. Part of this group circumnavigated the British Isles before returning to the Baltic. Inter-fleet transfers between the Northern, Baltic and Black Sea fleets continued and intensified. The exercises of 1964 saw the introduction of the latest missile-carrying warships; fleet strengths were increased and the scope and type of exercises between North Cape and the Faeroes Gap revealed more imagination and expertise.

The proliferation of Soviet nuclear attack submarines, and the consequent increased threat to American carrier task groups, led to the development of new escort vessels dedicated to anti-submarine warfare. Foremost among these were frigates, fitted with twin-shaft gas turbine engines with controllable-pitch propellers, giving them the power necessary to pursue high-speed nuclear-powered submarines. These vessels are at the cutting edge of naval technology, making their design and construction prohibitively costly for smaller navies, which usually prefer to buy them off the shelf from the principal maritime powers.

CRUISE MISSILE SUBMARINE

Development of the Soviet submarine fleet in the 1980s was impressive. In 1985, 10 submarine classes were under construction and two conversion programs were under way, culminating in the "Oscar"-class cruise missile submarine. The underwater equivalent of a *Kirov*-class cruiser, the first "Oscar I" class cruise missile submarine (SSGN) was laid down at Severodvinsk in 1978 and launched in the spring of 1980, starting sea trials later that year. The second was completed in 1982, and a third of the class–which became the first "Oscar II" completed in 1985, followed by a fourth, fifth and sixth at intervals of a year. The primary task of the "Oscar" class was to attack NATO carrier battle groups with a variety of submarine-launched cruise missiles. Perhaps the most famous "Oscar II" boat, for tragic reasons, was the *Kursk*.

Tarawa *was the first of five ships in a new class of general-purpose amphibious assault ships, and combined in one ship type the functions previously performed by four different types.*

The Visby *class was originally designed to be divided into two subcategories where some ships were optimized for surface combat and others for submarine hunting; however, this was changed due to cutbacks.*

DEFINITE PATTERN

The naval operations that took place in the latter years of the twentieth century, in support of UN-authorized actions in the Balkans, Afghanistan, Iraq and elsewhere, set a definite pattern for those that are likely to occur in the twenty-first. Sea warfare will never be the same again. The titanic mid-ocean battles that were a scenario of the Cold War will never be enacted. Instead, future naval battles will be fought along coastlines against developing countries or regional powers that present a threat to the international community, and for this reason diesel-electric submarines like the Dutch *Zeeleeuw*, and mine warfare vessels such as the *Tripartartite* minehunter, have assumed a new importance.

"The sea is a medium in which military and political power may be projected to critical areas of the world ... an activity associated largely with aircraft carriers and amphibious forces."

Hugh Faringdon, Military Analyst

Nautilus (SSN-571) 1954

The world's first nuclear-powered submarine was the American *Nautilus,* launched on January 21, 1954. Apart from her revolutionary propulsion system, she was designed along conventional lines. She became the first submarine to pass under the Arctic ice cap.

ESCAPE HATCH
The upper and lower hatches, as well as the escape door on one side, permitted several men at a time to make an emergency escape from the ship while submerged. The escape door also served as the torpedo loading hatch.

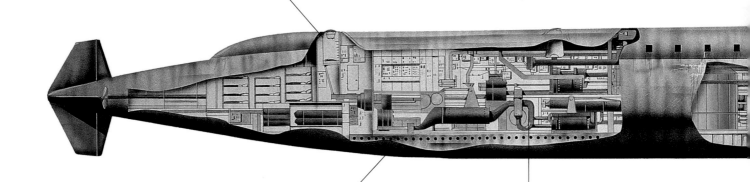

HULL
In order to avoid unnecessary risk, the hull was designed conventionally, with reactor safety being given absolute priority.

MACHINERY
Twin screws were driven by steam turbines using superheated steam generated by an S2W nuclear reactor via a heat exchanger.

- Launched on January 21, 1954; commissioned September 30 of the same year.

- First operational cruise, January 1955.

- First voyage under polar pack ice, August 1957.

- First successful voyage across the North Pole, August 1958.

- Decommissioned March 1980.

- Preserved as museum piece at Groton, Connecticut, 1982.

CONTROL CENTER
The Central Operating Compartment was the third compartment aft and was also divided into two levels. The Diving Stand, with aircraft-type controls, was located in the forward end of the compartment.

ARMAMENT
Nautilus was fitted with six 21-in (533-mm) bow torpedo tubes. The stowage racks for the torpedoes, known as "skids," were immediately aft of the tubes.

ACCOMMODATION
A partial deck divided the crew accommodations into two sections. The upper room was the officers' quarters, consisting of the wardroom, the pantry, and six staterooms. The crew's living area was below the officers' quarters.

NAUTILUS (SSN-571) – SPECIFICATION

Country of origin: USA
Type: Submarine
Laid down: June 14, 1952
Builder: General Dynamics
Launched: January 21, 1954
Commissioned: September 30, 1954
Decommissioned: March 3, 1980
Fate: Retained by navy as museum
Complement: 13 officers, 92 crew

Dimensions:
Displacement: (submerged) 4,092 tons (3,712 tonnes); (surface) 3,533 tons (3,205 tonnes)

Length: 320 ft (97.5 m)
Beam: 28 ft (8.5 m)
Draught: 26 ft (7.9 m)

Power plant:
Propulsion: Two-shaft nuclear steam turbines/electric motors producing 13,400 hp (10 MW)
Speed: 23 knots
Range: Unlimited

Armament:
Armament: 6 x 21-in (533-mm) torpedo tubes

Early trials with *Nautilus* established new records. This included travelling nearly 1,213 nm (2,245 km) submerged in 90 hours at 20 knots. At that time, this was the longest period spent underwater by an American submarine, as well as being the fastest speed submerged.

NAUTILUS

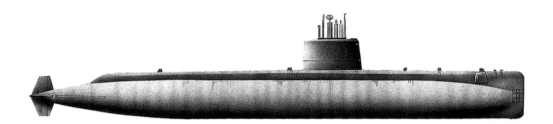

AMERICAN SSBN: *GEORGE WASHINGTON*

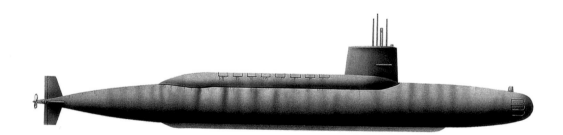

AMERICAN SSN: *SKATE*

AMERICAN SSN: *TRITON*

NAUTILUS AND SEAWOLF

There were in fact two prototype nuclear attack submarines. The other vessel, *Seawolf*, was launched in July 1955 and was the last U.S. submarine to feature a traditional conning tower, as distinct from the fin of later nuclear submarines. *Nautilus* was the more successful of the two. *Seawolf* was designed around the S2G nuclear reactor, intended as a backup to the S2W, but it had many operational problems and was replaced by an S2W in 1959. *Nautilus* was decommissioned in 1979 and preserved as a museum exhibit in 1982.

During the period July 22 to August 5, 1958, *Nautilus*, the world's first atomic-powered ship, added to her list of historic achievements by crossing the Arctic Ocean from the Bering Sea to the Greenland Sea, passing submerged beneath the geographic North Pole.

During the late 1940s, the major navies of the world made strenuous efforts, and carried out much experimentation, to find ways of improving the effectiveness of their submarine fleets. The U.S. Navy, however, was already forging ahead with developments that would revolutionize undersea warfare.

Work on a Submarine Thermal Reactor (STR), a nuclear reactor for submarines, began in 1948. It was developed by Westinghouse into the STR Mk 2 (later re-designated S2W) in collaboration with the Argonne National Laboratory, where key parts of the world's first atomic bomb had been established. Development of the associated technology was

Interior view

In operating conditions, a number of limitations in the design and construction of *Nautilus* became apparent, but these failings were corrected in subsequent submarines.

(1) Planesmen: *Nautilus* had two "planesmen," one operating the bow planes to control the boat's depth when submerged and one to control ascent and descent.

(2) Seating: The planesmen and helmsman, who sat between them, had the benefit of comfortable aircraft-type seats.

(3) Helmsman: As his name implies, the helmsman steered the boat both on the surface and underwater. To do this, he had to work closely with the planesmen.

(4) Instruments: For such a revolutionary craft, these were surprisingly simple, although most instruments, like the compass, had a backup.

(5) Speed: Built around a conventional hull form, *Nautilus* was limited to a top speed of about 20 knots.

(6) Gyrocompass: Navigation beneath the Arctic ice sheet was difficult. A gyrocompass was installed to aid the boat's passage.

Nautilus *is shown here about to berth in a French port during her Mediterranean deployment. The French yachts in the background are decked with bunting as a sign of welcome.*

the responsibility of a team of scientists and engineers at the Naval Reactors Branch of the Atomic Energy Commission, led by an energetic U.S. Navy officer, Captain Hyman G. Rickover. On December 12, 1951, when the Department of the Navy was satisfied that the STR was a viable proposition, the U.S. Navy decided to order a hull for the new reactor. The name chosen for the revolutionary new boat was *Nautilus*, which commemorated not only two previous U.S. submarines, but also Robert Fulton's submersible of 1800 and the fictional boat in Jules Verne's book *Twenty Thousand Leagues Under the Sea.*

The keel of the latest *Nautilus* was laid by President Truman at the Electric Boat Division of General Dynamics in Groton, Connecticut, on June 14, 1952. Work progressed rapidly, the *Nautilus* (SSN-571) being launched on January 21, 1954, and commissioned eight months later.

From 1955–57, *Nautilus* underwent various trials to investigate the effects of increased submarine speeds and endurance. On February 4, 1957, she logged her 60,000th nautical mile, matching the endurance of Jules Verne's fictional vessel, and in May she deployed to the Pacific to take part in exercises with the Pacific Fleet. Later in the year she toured NATO naval bases in the North Atlantic area and participated in NATO exercises, which demonstrated that most of the methods of submarine detection then in use were virtually ineffective against a nuclear-powered vessel.

"*NAUTILUS* NINETY DEGREES NORTH"

In July 1958 she sailed north from Pearl Harbor in the Pacific and passed under the polar ice cap, an achievement marked by the historic signal "*Nautilus* Ninety Degrees North" sent to the U.S. Admiralty by her skipper, Commander William R. Anderson. She carried on from the North Pole and, after 96 hours and 1,590 nm (2,945 km) under the ice, surfaced northeast of Greenland, having completed the first successful submerged voyage across the roof of the world.

The journey had not been without its dangers. In the Bering Strait, ice extended as much as 60 ft (18 m) below sea level. During the initial attempt to traverse the Bering Strait, there was insufficient room for the submarine to pass between the ice and the sea bottom. During the second, successful attempt, the submarine passed through a known channel close to Alaska, a route taken in order to avoid detection and the ice.

Long Beach (CGN-9) 1959

The first U.S. surface warship to be powered by nuclear energy, *Long Beach* was originally intended to be no larger than a frigate. However, during the design stage she rapidly reached the dimensions of a heavy cruiser.

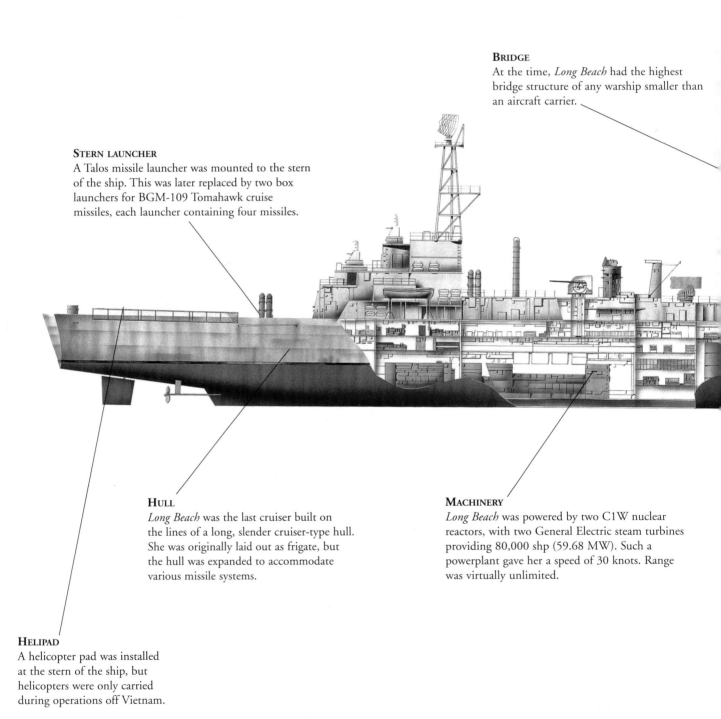

BRIDGE
At the time, *Long Beach* had the highest bridge structure of any warship smaller than an aircraft carrier.

STERN LAUNCHER
A Talos missile launcher was mounted to the stern of the ship. This was later replaced by two box launchers for BGM-109 Tomahawk cruise missiles, each launcher containing four missiles.

HULL
Long Beach was the last cruiser built on the lines of a long, slender cruiser-type hull. She was originally laid out as frigate, but the hull was expanded to accommodate various missile systems.

MACHINERY
Long Beach was powered by two C1W nuclear reactors, with two General Electric steam turbines providing 80,000 shp (59.68 MW). Such a powerplant gave her a speed of 30 knots. Range was virtually unlimited.

HELIPAD
A helicopter pad was installed at the stern of the ship, but helicopters were only carried during operations off Vietnam.

SUPERSTRUCTURE
The high box-like superstructure housed the SCANFAR radar system, comprising the AN/SPS-32 and AN/SPS-33 phased array radars.

FORWARD LAUNCHERS
There were two forward launchers for the Terrier and Talos surface-to-air missiles. These were later replaced by the longer-range Standard missile.

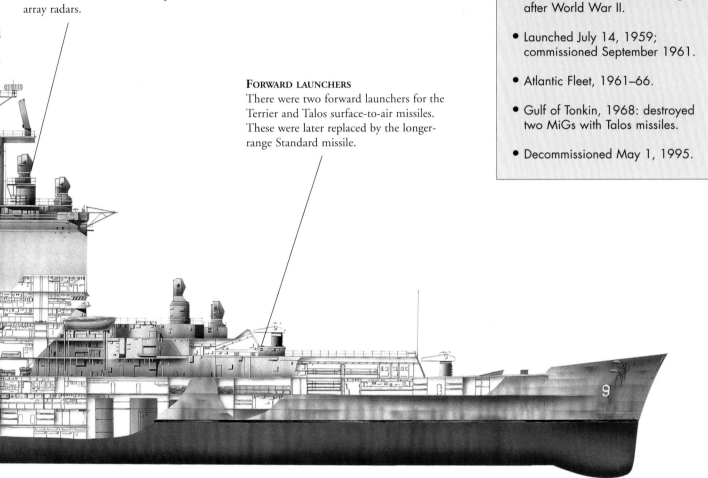

LONG BEACH (CGN-9) – SPECIFICATION

Country of origin: USA
Type: Missile cruiser
Laid down: December 2, 1957
Builder: Bethlehem Steel Co., Fore River Shipyard, Massachusetts
Launched: July 14, 1959
Commissioned: September 9, 1961
Decommissioned: May 1, 1995
Fate: Struck May 1, 1995
Complement: 1,160 officers and men

Dimensions:
Displacement: (standard) 15,540 tons (14,098 tonnes); (full) 17,525 tons (15,898 tonnes)
Length: 721 ft 3 in (220 m); **Beam:** 71 ft 6 in (21.79 m);
   Draught: (30 ft 7 in (9.32 m)

Power plant:
Propulsion: 2 C1W nuclear reactors, 2 General Electric turbines producing 80,000 shp (59.68 MW)
Speed: 30 knots
Range: Unlimited

Armament & Armor:
Armament: 2 x 5-in (127-mm) Mk 30 guns; 2 x Mk 10 missile launchers Standard missiles (ER), 2 x Mk 141 Harpoon missile launchers; 1 x Mk 16 ASROC missile launcher; Mk 46 torpedoes from two Mk 32 triple mounts; 2 x 0.79-in (20-mm) Phalanx CIWS; 2 x armored box launchers for Tomahawk cruise missiles
Armor: N/A
Aircraft: None. Helicopter launch pad

Long Beach was the third ship to be named after the city of Long Beach, California. The first was a converted German cargo ship, seized in 1917, and the second was a patrol frigate, which had served in the U.S. Navy from 1943–45.

AMERICAN GUIDED MISSILE CRUISER: *LEAHY*

LONG BEACH

In May 1964, *Long Beach* joined the nuclear-powered aircraft carrier *Enterprise* (CVN-65) and the guided missile frigate *Bainbridge* (DLGN-25) to form the all-nuclear-powered Task Force 1, the first such battle force of its kind in the history of naval operations. At the end of July, the three warships began Operation Sea Orbit, a two-month unrefuelled cruise around the world. The task force left Gibraltar on July 31, sailed down the Atlantic and around Africa, across the Indian and Pacific Oceans and around Cape Horn, completing the 30,216 nm (55,793 km) voyage in 65 days.

AMERICAN GUIDED MISSILE CRUISER: *BELKNAP*

AMERICAN AIR DEFENSE CRUISER: *TICONDEROGA*

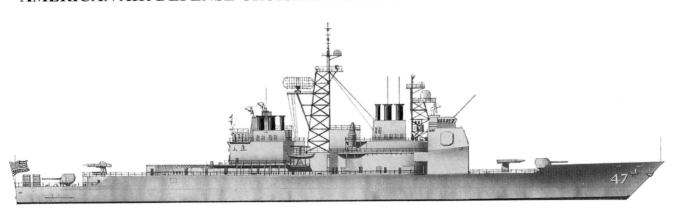

Long Beach (CGN-9) was the first U.S. surface warship powered by nuclear energy. During the Vietnam War in 1967–68, her long-range TaLOS SAM systems engaged North Vietnamese MiGs on several occasions.

Long Beach was a one-ship class. The reason for this was that she was an experimental platform for her phased array radar system, a precursor of the AN/SPY-1 system installed in later Aegis guided-missile warships.

In 1966, *Long Beach* deployed to the Western Pacific for her first tour of duty off Vietnam. She was stationed mainly in the northern part of the Gulf of Tonkin, where the U.S. Navy had created a Positive Identification Radar Advisory Zone (PIRAZ). From this position she maintained constant radar surveillance to ensure that North Vietnamese intruder aircraft did not evade identification by attempting to mingle with returning U.S. strike aircraft. *Long Beach* also provided facilities for an on-board search-and-rescue helicopter. During this initial tour, one of her Air Intercept Controllers (AIC) directed a U.S. Navy F-4 Phantom to shoot down an Antonov An-2 Colt aircraft that was attempting to engage South Vietnamese naval craft.

Long Beach returned to the USA in July 1967 and returned to the Gulf of Tonkin in 1968. During this deployment, her Talos missiles destroyed two North

Vietnamese MiG-17s at a range of 70 miles (112 km). This was the first recorded use, in combat conditions, of naval surface-to-air missiles.

COMPASSIONATE RESCUE DUTIES

After Vietnam, *Long Beach* carried out routine duties in the Western Pacific, and in 1975 she was part of the task force assembled to rescue American seamen captured by the Khmer Rouge when their ship was seized. In 1980, she was involved in the rescue of 114 Vietnamese "boat people," fleeing the Communist regime.

As a result of experiences in the Vietnam War, in 1968, a conventional SPS-12 air search radar was fitted to *Long Beach* in order to supplement her fixed arrays. In 1970, an integral Identification Friend/Foe (IFF) and digital Talos fire-control system were fitted to the ship as well.

By 1979 the Talos system was growing obsolete, so the launchers and radars were removed and two quadruple Harpoon surface-to-surface missile launchers were installed. In the following year the fixed-array radar systems (which had proved less than adequate) were removed and replaced by SPS-48 and SPS-49 radars, the original planar array panels on the superstructure being replaced by armor plate.

In 1981 the Terrier missiles were replaced by Standard SM-2ER SAMs, and two armored box launchers for Tomahawk cruise missiles were installed in 1986, the Harpoons being repositioned along the superstructure to make room. Kevlar armor and a Tactical Flag Command Center were also fitted. For additional defense, two Phalanx Close-In Weapon Systems (CIWS) were added.

In 1987, *Long Beach* provided support during Operation Nimble Archer. In this operation American warships attacked Iranian oil platforms that were allegedly being used by Iranian forces as command-and-control posts with radars to track shipping in the area and that had been equipped with communications gear to relay messages between the mainland and Iranian forces operating near the platforms. Then, in 1991, *Long Beach* operated as part of the UN task force during Operation Desert Storm.

AWAITING RECYCLING

Long Beach was deactivated on May 1, 1995, having seen more than 33 years of operational service. By the year 2010, she was still awaiting recycling at the Puget Sound Naval Shipyard, in Bremerton, Washington.

Close-up

Long Beach was propelled by two nuclear reactors – one for each propeller shaft – and was capable of speeds in excess of 30 knots.

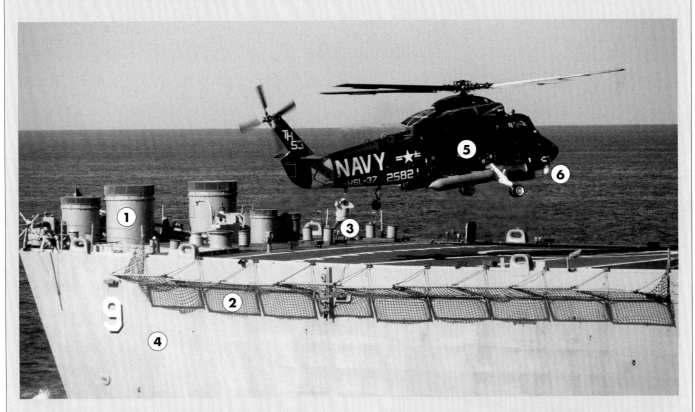

(1) **Launcher:** The rear launcher for the Talos was replaced with two Tomahawk cruise missile box launchers. Each launcher held 4 missiles.

(2) **Safety nets:** These were an essential feature around a helicopter landing pad, as protection against the powerful downwash from the rotor blades.

(3) **Crewman:** A crewman in a distinctive yellow jacket guides the helicopter down to a spot landing.

(4) **Hull:** *Long Beach* was designed as an "all-missile" ship from the very beginning. She was also the last cruiser built on a traditional long, lean cruiser hull.

(5) **Helicopter:** The one seen here is a Kaman SH-2 Sea Sprite, which had both anti-submarine and anti-surface-vessel warfare capabilities.

(6) **Helicopter scanner:** The SH-2Fs were fitted with a forward-looking infrared scanner under the nose.

Resolution 1966

In February 1963 the British government stated its intention to order four or five *Resolution*-class nuclear-powered ballistic missile submarines, armed with the American Polaris SLBM, to take over the British nuclear deterrent role from the RAF in 1968.

ELECTRONICS
The vessel was fitted with one Type 1007 surface-search radar, one Type 2001 bow sonar, one Type 2007 sonar, one Type 2023 retractable towed-array sonar, one Type 2019 intercept sonar, and one ESM suite, as well as extensive communications equipment.

TORPEDO TUBES
Although designed for strategic missile attack, the *Resolution*-class boats were fitted with six 21-in (533-mm) torpedo tubes in the forward part of the hull.

HULL
The hull was assembled on the berth from sections prefabricated in the assembly shop. The fore and aft parts of the ship were built up simultaneously, the prefabricated missile sections, complete with missile tubes, being fitted into the space between.

CREW
Normal crew on *Resolution* was 154. Each Ship Submersible Ballistic Nuclear (SSBN) had two crews, known as "port" and "starboard," alternating on each voyage of approximately three months' duration.

MISSILES

Resolution had launch tubes for each of her 16 Polaris A3 SLBMs. Her Polaris system was updated in 1984 with the Chevaline IFE (Improved Front End). This included two new warheads and re-entry bodies, as well as super-hardened penetration aids to resist anti-ballistic missile (ABM) attack, replacing the original three ET.317 warheads.

MACHINERY

Resolution's power plant was a pressurized water-cooled reactor powering two steam turbines driving a single shaft, giving the boat a speed of at least 25 knots underwater.

F A C T S

- Launched September 15, 1966; commissioned October 2, 1967.

- First live firing of Polaris missile, February 15, 1968.

- First operational patrol, June 15, 1968.

- Carried out 69 operational patrols, including one of 108 days (in 1991).

- Decommissioned October 22, 1994; laid up at Rosyth.

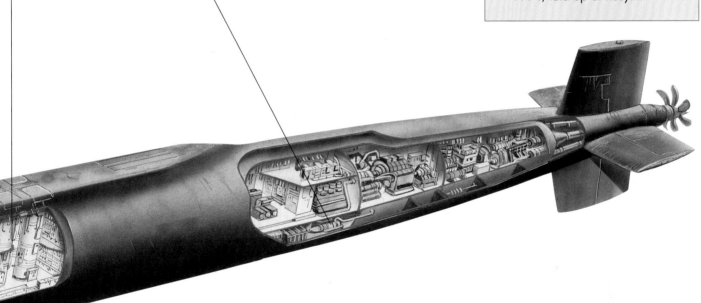

RESOLUTION – SPECIFICATION

Country of origin: United Kingdom
Type: Submarine
Laid down: February 26, 1964
Builder: Vickers Shipbuilding Ltd., Barrow-in-Furness, England
Launched: September 15, 1966
Commissioned: October 2, 1967
Decommissioned: October 22, 1994
Fate: Laid up at Rosyth Dockyard, Scotland
Complement: 143

Dimensions:
Displacement: (surfaced) 7,500 tons (6,804 tonnes); (submerged) 8,400 tons (7,620 tonne)
Length: 425 ft (130 m); **Beam:** 33 ft (10 m);
    Draught: 30 ft 1 in (9.17 m)

Power plant:
Propulsion: 1 x Vickers/Rolls-Royce PWR.1 pressurized-water nuclear reactor, 2 steam turbines
Speed: (surface) 20 knots; (submerged) 25 knots
Range: Unlimited

Armament:
Armament: 16 x Polaris A3TK IRBMs; 6 x 21-in (533-mm) torpedo tubes

Resolution was the first of four similar vessels in her class. The second, *Repulse*, followed in September 1968, with *Renown* and *Revenge* following in November 1968 and December 1969, respectively.

U.S. SSBN: *LAFAYETTE*

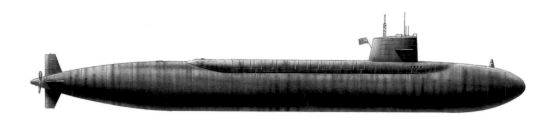

BRITISH SSN: *VALIANT*

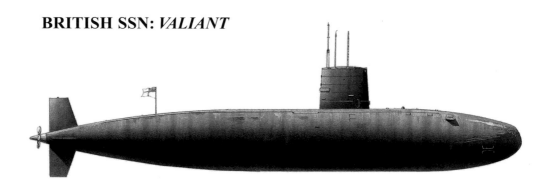

BRITISH SSBN: *"R" CLASS*

BRITISH SSN: *DREADNOUGHT*

POLARIS MISSILES

The project to develop the Polaris SLBM began in the mid-1950s and, at the time, was considered extremely ambitious. The weapon became operational in 1960, the original missile being the Polaris A-1 with a single 0.5 MT warhead. In 1962 the A-2 missile was introduced, with more powerful rocket motors and better in-flight control; the A-3 appeared in 1974, with more powerful fuel, better guidance, and multiple warheads. *Resolution*'s Polaris system originally had three ET.17 warheads mounted on each missile, but this was updated in 1984 with the Chevaline IFE (Improved Front End) system. This included new warhead re-entry bodies, with penetration aids super-hardened to resist ABM attack.

A Royal Navy Sea King helicopter winches up a crewman from the deck of Resolution. *Exchanges of personnel, and sometimes the evacuation of sick personnel, by helicopter were not uncommon.*

The design, construction, and deployment of the *Resolution* class was claimed to have been the only British defense procurement program to have been completed under budget.

Resolution (S22) was the first of a class of four ballistic missile submarines built for the Royal Navy. She was based on the U.S. Navy's *Lafayette* class. These submarines allowed the Royal Navy to assume a Quick Reaction Alert (QRA) posture, taking over responsibility for Great Britain's strategic nuclear deterrent from the RAF's Blue Steel-armed Vulcan and Victor V-Bomber force, as agreed at the 1962 Nassau Conference. The four submarines (a fifth was cancelled) used U.S. Polaris missiles, missile tubes, and fire control systems plus British engines and other equipment.

Resolution's keel was laid down at the Vickers yard, Barrow-in-Furness, on February 26, 1964. Colossal planning and design effort went into the Polaris submarine program, which involved half a million man-hours of planning. More than 10,000 carefully detailed drawings were prepared, all of

which had to be translated into the physical business of construction. Additionally, a full-scale wooden "mock-up" was built. Not only did this allow the exact positioning of any piece of equipment to be planned and the routes for cables, pipes, and trunking to be decided upon, but it enabled crew to undergo training and become familiar with their new boat before they even set foot on her.

PROGRAM POLITICALLY CURTAILED

The British Polaris boats lacked the fin-mounted diving planes of the original *Lafayette*s, and instead borrowed certain features from the British *Valiant* class of nuclear attack submarines. To guarantee that one submarine would always remain on patrol, the Royal Navy planned to build a fifth submarine. However, it was cancelled by the incoming Labor government in 1964 as an economic measure and to placate those calling for nuclear disarmament. Officially, there was never a gap in submarine QRA patrols. Unofficially, it is believed that the RAF's Vulcans took back the strategic deterrent commitment on at least one occasion in the late 1960s.

Launched in September 1966, *Resolution* was completed in October 1967, and went on her first patrol in 1968 as planned after completing live firing trials with Polaris off of Florida. To improve the ability of the Polaris missile to penetrate the USSR's increasingly sophisticated anti-ballistic missile (ABM) defenses, Britain embarked on an expensive and ambitious upgrade program code-named Chevaline, adding decoys to the Polaris warhead.

New Trident-armed *Vanguard*s replaced the *Resolution*-class submarines starting in 1995. *Revenge* was withdrawn in 1992, and *Resolution* followed in 1994. The remaining two submarines in the class were withdrawn during 1995–96.

Interior view

The four *Resolution* class SSBNs (Ship Submersible Ballistic Nuclear) served the Royal Navy well, but after 20 years in service suffered problems with their reactors.

(1) Confined space: Crew members spend months underwater in a confined space, and find that it takes days for their eyes to adjust to long distance again.

(2) Bombers: In the Royal Navy, ballistic missile submarines are referred to as "bombers."

(3) Modern ballistic missile submarines are usually designed to launch their weapons at keel depth, typically less than 164 ft (50 m).

(4) Features: The *Resolution* class incorporated several enviable features, such as a machinery loading hatch, automated hovering system, and welded hull valves.

(5) Construction: The construction was unusual in that the bow and stern were constructed separately before being assembled together.

(6) Design: This was a modification of the *Valiant*-class fleet submarine, extended to incorporate the missile compartment between the fin and the nuclear reactor.

Nimitz (CVN-68) 1972

The *Nimitz*-class nuclear-powered supercarriers, in service with the U.S. Navy, are the largest capital ships in the world. The ship was named for Fleet Admiral Chester W. Nimitz, who commanded the U.S. Pacific Fleet in World War II.

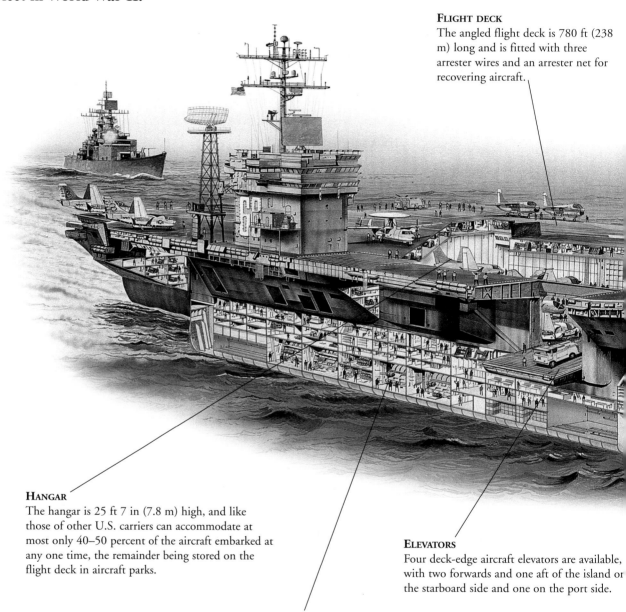

FLIGHT DECK
The angled flight deck is 780 ft (238 m) long and is fitted with three arrester wires and an arrester net for recovering aircraft.

HANGAR
The hangar is 25 ft 7 in (7.8 m) high, and like those of other U.S. carriers can accommodate at most only 40–50 percent of the aircraft embarked at any one time, the remainder being stored on the flight deck in aircraft parks.

ELEVATORS
Four deck-edge aircraft elevators are available, with two forwards and one aft of the island on the starboard side and one on the port side.

MACHINERY
Nimitz is powered by two Westinghouse A4W nuclear reactors and four steam turbines, generating 260,000 shp (194 MW).

FACTS

- Launched May 13, 1972; commissioned May 1975.

- The *Nimitz* reaches more than 23 stories high from the keel to the top of the mast.

- First deployment to the Mediterranean, July 1976, with Carrier Air Wing 8 embarked.

- Built to have an active service life of at least 50 years.

- There are 10 *Nimitz*-class carriers, the last of which (CVN-77 *George H.W. Bush*) was commissioned in 2009.

COMPLEMENT

Nimitz has a complement of 3,200, plus a further 2,480 manning the air group. The *Nimitz* can stock at least 70 days' supply of refrigerated and dry storage goods. The Food Services Department can provide 18,000–20,000 meals a day.

AIRCRAFT

Nimitz's Carrier Air Wing includes four squadrons of F/A-18 Hornets/Super Hornets, an electronic attack squadron with EA-8B Prowlers, an early warning squadron with E-2C Hawkeyes, and an ASW squadron with SH-60 helicopters.

NIMITZ (CVN-68) – SPECIFICATION

Country of origin: USA
Type: Supercarrier
Laid down: July 22, 1968
Builder: Newport News Shipbuilding
Launched: May 13, 1972
Commissioned: May 3, 1975 (still in service)
Complement: Ship's company: 3,200; Air wing: 2,480

Dimensions:
Displacement: 113,120 tons (102,621 tonnes)
Length: 1,092 ft (332.8 m)
Beam: 252 ft (76.8 m)
Draught: 37 ft (11.3 m)

Power plant:
Propulsion: 2 x Westinghouse A4W nuclear reactors, quadruple shafts producing 260,000 shp (194 MW)
Speed: 31.5 knots
Range: Unlimited

Armament & Armor:
Armament: 2 x 21-cell Sea RAM; 2 x MK29 Sea Sparrow
Armor: Classified
Aircraft: 90 fixed-wing and helicopters

Nimitz-class carriers have a formidable nuclear-strike capability. Their magazines are capable of accommodating more than 100 nuclear weapons for tasks ranging from anti-submarine warfare to area attacks on cities.

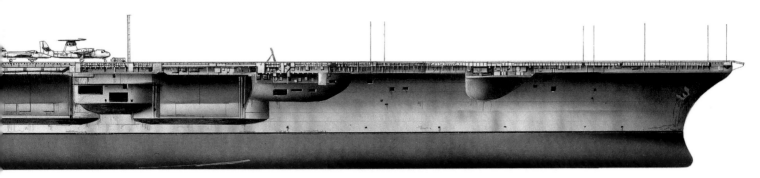

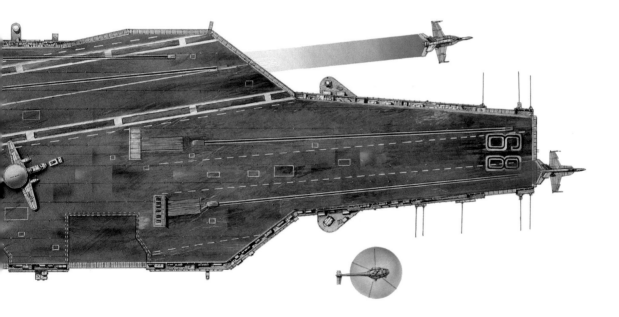

NIMITZ

In time of war, the Mediterranean-based U.S. Sixth Fleet would make an important, and probably decisive, contribution to the security of NATO's southern flank. The fleet has eight task forces, covering the whole spectrum of warfare from air strike through amphibious assault to submarine attack. At the heart of the whole organization is the Battle Force. In the case of the Sixth Fleet, this is Task Force 60, which comprises two carriers – a nuclear-powered attack carrier, usually a vessel of the *Nimitz* class, and a smaller attack carrier. The larger attack carriers have an air group of 90–95 aircraft, the smaller vessels about 75 aircraft.

An aircraft carrier like Nimitz *is at the core of an extremely powerful battle group, comprising almost every type of warship, including nuclear attack submarines, which protect its flanks.*

The aircraft carrier is a powerful element of U.S. foreign policy. Former president Bill Clinton once said that the first thing any president asked when being told of a new crisis anywhere in the world was, "Where are the nearest carriers?"

The first three *Nimitz*-class carriers were originally designed as replacements for the elderly *Midway* class. They differed from the earlier *Enterprise* in having a new two-reactor power plant design in two separate compartments, with the ordnance magazines between and forward of them. This increased the internal space available to allow the carrier to accommodate some 2,570 tons (2,331 tonnes) of aviation weapons and 2.8 million gallons (10.6 million liters) of aircraft fuel, enough for 16 days of continuous flight operations before the stocks need to be replenished.

WORLDWIDE DUTIES
Commissioned in May 1975, *Nimitz* deployed to the Mediterranean in July 1976, with Carrier Air Wing 8

embarked. It was to be the first of several deployments to the Mediterranean and the Middle East. On her third deployment, in 1979–80, she moved to the Indian Ocean and conducted Operation Evening Light, in which her helicopters made an abortive attempt to rescue 52 American hostages held in the U.S. Embassy at Tehran, Iran.

Her sixth and final deployment to the Mediterranean took place in 1986, after which she proceeded to a new station in the Western Pacific. In 1988 she returned to the Middle East and operated in the North Arabian Sea on tanker protection duty, and in February 1991 she deployed to the Persian Gulf, where she relieved *Ranger* in the aftermath of Operation Desert Storm.

In 1996 she returned to the Pacific, patrolling the waters around Taiwan in a show of strength as the Chinese People's Republic conducted missile tests in the area. In the following year she made an around-the-world cruise that ended at Newport News, Virginia, in March 1998. She remained there for the next three years, undergoing an extensive overhaul.

The next decade was a busy one for *Nimitz*. In March 2003 she sailed on her eleventh operational deployment, during which her air group supported operations in Iraq and Afghanistan. On January 24, 2008, *Nimitz* deployed to the Western Pacific, and on February 9 two Russian Tu-142 aircraft overflew the carrier while she was on station. Four F/A-18s were launched when the Russian aircraft were 500 miles (800 km) away from the U.S. ships, and intercepted them 50 miles (80 km) south of *Nimitz*. Two F/A-18s trailed one of the aircraft, which buzzed the deck of the carrier twice, while the other two F/A-18s trailed another Tu-142 circling about 50 miles (80 km) away from the carrier. Reportedly, there was no radio communication between the U.S. and

Russian aircraft. According to the U.S. Department of Defense, one of the two aircraft was said to have flown above *Nimitz* at an altitude of 2,000 ft (610 m). On the same day, Russian aircraft entered Japanese airspace, causing the Japanese to protest to Russia's ambassador in Tokyo. Again, on March 5, 2008, a Russian maritime surveillance Tu-142 came within 3–5 nm (5/6–9.3 km) and flew 2000 ft (610 m) above *Nimitz* and her battle group. Two F/A-18 fighters intercepted the Russian aircraft and escorted it out of the area.

In 2009, the *Nimitz* was once again operating in support of Enduring Freedom, the NATO operation in Afghanistan.

Interior view

An aircraft carrier flight deck is one of the most exhilarating and dangerous work environments in the world. Smooth operations depend on tight and meticulous control.

(1) **Directing flight: In the Primary Flight Control (Pri-Fly), the air officer (left) and air officer assistant (right) direct all aircraft on the flight deck and within an 5-mile (8-km) radius.**

(2) **Equipment: The air officer and air officer assistant have an array of computers and communications equipment.**

(3) **View: The excellent view along the entire flight deck, facilitated by extensive windows, aids in directing aircraft activity.**

(4) **Landing signals officer: When an approaching aircraft comes within 0.75 miles (1.2 km), the landing signals officers take over control to direct the landing.**

(5) **Vulture's row: At the same level as the Pri-Fly, crew visitors can walk out onto "vulture's row," a balcony platform with a view of the flight deck.**

(6) **At the next level down from Pri-Fly, the captain directs the ship from the bridge.**

Tarawa (LHA-1) 1973

The primary mission of the LHA-1 *Tarawa* class is to land and sustain U.S. Marines on any shore during combat operations. The ships provide the nucleus of a multi-ship Amphibious Readiness Group (ARG).

FLIGHT DECK
The flight deck has nine landings spots. The carrier-type island is to starboard, with the helicopter elevators to port. The flight deck can handle 10 helicopters simultaneously.

AIRCRAFT
The *Tarawa*-class vessels can support 35 aircraft, including AV-8B Harrier IIs, helicopter gunships, and heavy lift and assault helicopters.

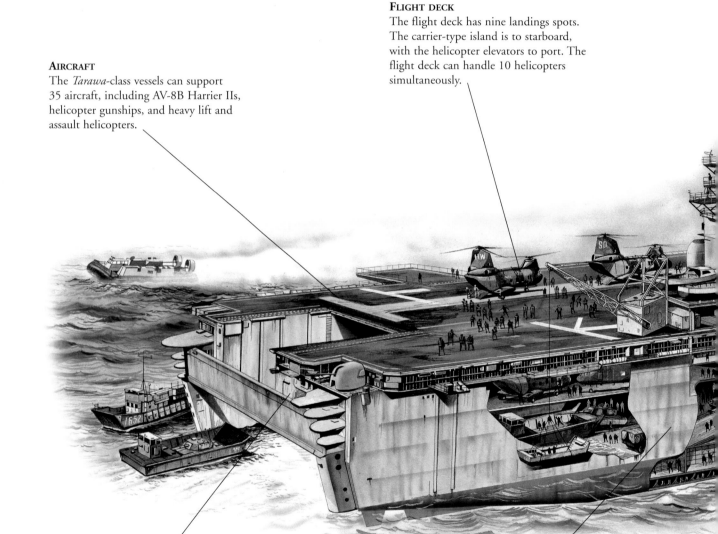

WELL DECK
There is a large well deck in the stern of the ship for a number of amphibious assault craft, including air cushion vehicles. The well deck accommodates up to four LCU 1610 or one LCAC or seven LCM(8) or 17 LCM(6) landing craft.

MACHINERY
The *Tarawa* class is powered by two steam turbines delivering a total of 70,000 shp (52.2 MW) and giving a range of 10,000 miles (18,520 km) at 20 knots. The propulsion system is highly automated.

ACCOMMODATIONS

The ships can accommodate an average of 960 officers and men and more than 2,000 marines. All troops have bunks, and the ships are air-conditioned throughout.

COMMUNICATIONS

Communications systems include SRR-1, WSC-3 UHF, WSC-6 SHF, and USC-38 SHF SATCOM receivers, and an SMQ-11 weather satellite receiver.

FACTS

- Named after Tarawa Atoll in the Pacific, captured by U.S. Marines after bitter fighting in 1943.

- Launched December 1, 1973; commissioned May 1976.

- First deployment 1979, with AV-8 Harrier V/STOL aircraft embarked.

- Flagship of amphibious task force in Operation Desert Storm, 1991.

- Deployed in support of Operation Iraqi Freedom, 2005–06.

- Decommissioned March 31, 2009.

TARAWA (LHA-1) – SPECIFICATION

Country of origin: USA
Type: Amphibious assault ship
Laid down: November 15, 1971
Builder: Ingalls Shipbuilding
Launched: December 1, 1973
Commissioned: May 29, 1976
Decommissioned: March 31, 2009
Fate: Awaiting disposal
Complement: Over 960 crew and over 2,000 marines

Dimensions:
Displacement: 38,900 tons (35,289 tonnes)
Length: 820 ft (250 m); **Beam:** 106 ft (32 m);
  Draught: 26 ft (7.9 m)

Power plant:
Propulsion: Two shaft, two geared steam turbines, 70,000 shp (52.2 MW)
Speed: 24 knots
Range: 10,000 nm (18,520 km) at 20 knots

Armor & Armament:
Armament: 4 x Mk 38 Mod 1 0.98-in (25-mm) Bushmaster cannons, 5 x 0.5in (20.7-mm) M2HB Browning MGs, 2 x 0.98-in (20-mm) x Mk 15 Phalanx (CIWS), 2 x Mk 49 RAM launchers
Aircraft: Up to 35 helicopters, 8 AV-8B Harrier II VSTOL aircraft

Tarawa was the first of five ships in a new class of general-purpose amphibious assault ships, and combined the functions previously performed by four different types: the Amphibious Assault Ship (LPH); the Amphibious Transport Dock (LPD); the Amphibious Cargo Ship (LKA); and the Dock Landing Ship (LSD).

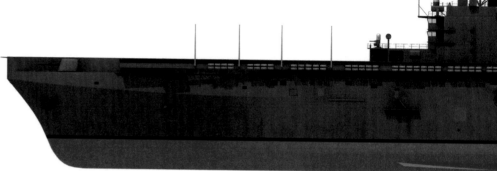

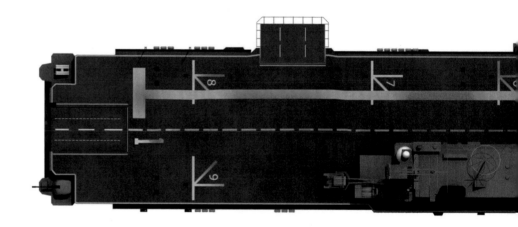

TARAWA'S COMPUTER

The nerve center of the *Tarawa* class is a tactical amphibious warfare computer, which keeps track of the landing force's positions after leaving the ship, and also tracks enemy targets ashore. The tactical data system can also direct the targeting of the guns and missiles from the ship as well as the support ships. The system maintains air and surface traffic control during the landing phase for the ship's own helicopters, and also provides direction for the task force's supporting ships and assault craft, and for combat air patrols.

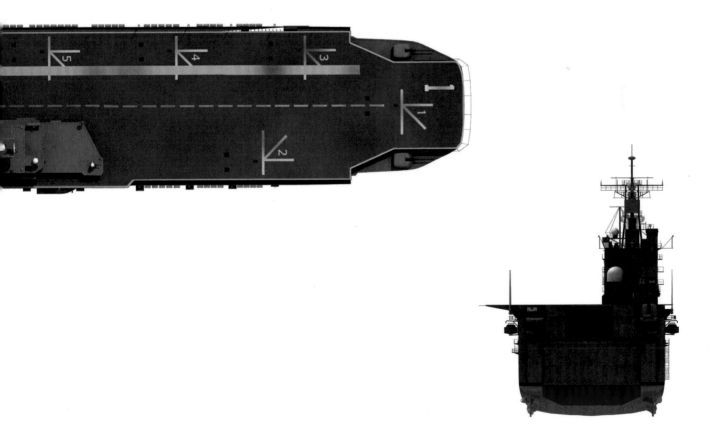

The other ships in the *Tarawa* class were *Saipan*, *Belleau Wood*, *Nassau*, and *Peleliu*. All but the last two ships have been decommissioned.

Tarawa's first deployment took place in 1978, when she spent a period working with her AV-8 Harriers. During this time, she rescued 400 Vietnamese refugees from the South China Sea. Her operations took her worldwide, and 1983 found her in the Mediterranean, where she supported UN peacekeepers in Beirut, Lebanon.

In December 1990, *Tarawa* acted as the flagship of an amphibious assault force consisting of 13 vessels placed off of Iraqi-occupied Kuwait. In January and February of 1991 she took part in a successful deception exercise when her marines landed in Saudi Arabia just outside the border of Kuwait to divert attention from the real Coalition attack, which was to be an armored thrust through the desert. Her contribution to Operation Desert Storm was quickly followed by a humanitarian mission to cyclone-torn Bangladesh in May 1991, when she supplied rice and equipment for purifying water to the local people.

Interior view

Tarawa is equipped with a 300-bed hospital, four medical operating rooms, and three dental operating rooms.

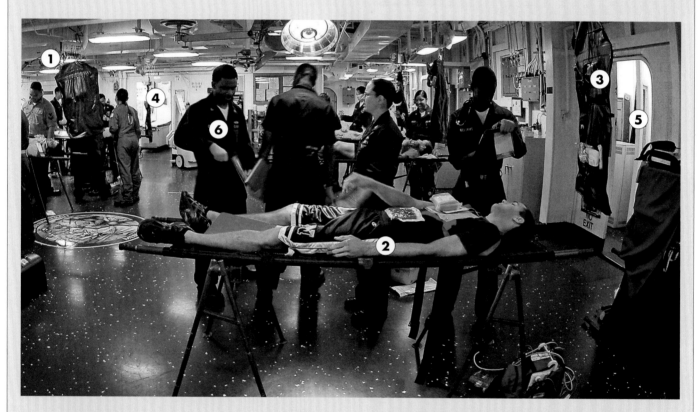

(1) **Medical facilities:** The hospital was fitted out to the same standard as the finest local hospitals in the U.S.

(2) **Exercises:** Emergency exercises are carried out frequently in the hospital to maintain a state of readiness.

(3) **Dental care:** The mission of the dental department was to provide care for active duty Navy and Marine Corps personnel to prevent or remedy diseases.

(4) **Laboratory:** This was equipped with a chemistry analyzer, coulter counter, automated blood gas analyzer, and microbiology capability.

(5) **Freezer:** *Tarawa*'s freezers could store 1,000 units of frozen blood and could process six units every 30 minutes for emergency use.

(6) The medical staff consists of one general medical officer (department head), one medical administrative officer (division officer), and sixteen other technicians.

Following four and a half months of providing the setting for intensive individual ship and amphibious refresher training for embarked marines,
Tarawa *ended 1978 in her home port of San Diego, California, on Christmas stand-down.*

In May 1992, *Tarawa* deployed for the eighth time to the Western Pacific, and entered the Indian Ocean to participate in a joint U.S./Kuwaiti exercise. The ship also supported the insertion of Pakistani troops into Somalia in support of UN humanitarian relief, and returned to San Diego in November 1992. Her 1992 deployment included visits to Hong Kong, Singapore, the Persian Gulf, Somalia, and Australia.

In April 1996, following an extensive overhaul at Long Beach, California, *Tarawa* set out on her ninth Western Pacific and Indian Ocean deployment, in the course of which she carried out amphibious training exercises with the navies of Thailand, Saudi Arabia, and Jordan. She also helped enforce the "no-fly" zone over southern Iraq, and participated in Operation Desert Strike, a U.S. response to an Iraqi offensive in Kurdistan in 1996.

SUPPORT IN TIMES OF CRISIS

Tarawa was passing through the Strait of Hormuz in the middle of October 2000 on her way into the Persian Gulf when the *Arleigh Burke*-class destroyer *Cole* was attacked by suicide bombers using an inflatable craft.

Upon being notified of the attack, *Tarawa* came about and steamed full ahead to the Port of Aden in Yemen, where she joined *Donald Cook*, *Hawes*, and the Royal Navy frigate *Marlborough*, already providing logistical support and harbor security, as the command ship in charge of force protection. *Tarawa* remained with *Cole* until she was secure aboard the Norwegian heavy-lift semi-submersible salvage ship *Blue Marlin* for passage to the U.S. *Tarawa* then returned to duty in the Persian Gulf.

A further deployment in 2005 again took *Tarawa* by way of the Pacific to the Persian Gulf, where she delivered the 13th Marine Expeditionary Unit to Iraq in support of Operation Iraqi Freedom.

Tarawa was decommissioned at San Diego Naval Base, California, on March 31, 2009. She was the second ship to bear the name. The original *Tarawa* was commissioned in December 1945, too late to serve in World War II. In the early 1950s, she was redesignated an attack carrier (CVA) and then an antisubmarine warfare carrier (CVS). Except for one tour in the Far East, she spent her entire second career operating in the Atlantic and Caribbean.

LOS ANGELES (SSN 688) 1974

The *Los Angeles* class is the mainstay of the U.S. Navy's attack submarine fleet. The vessels in this class are very large, weighing in at about 2,000 tons (1,800 tonnes) more than their predecessors, the *Sturgeon* class.

COMPARTMENTS
There are two watertight compartments in the *Los Angeles* class. The forward compartment contains spaces for the crew to live, for weapons handling, and control spaces. The aft compartment contains the bulk of the ship's engineering systems.

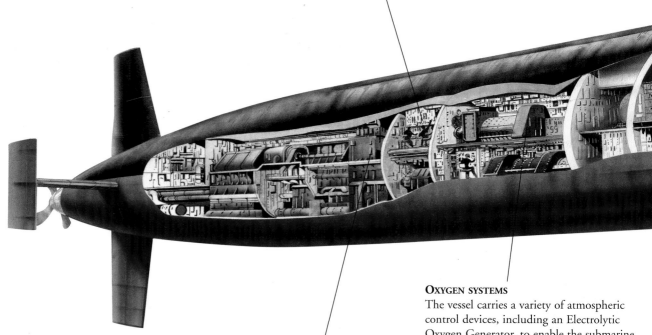

OXYGEN SYSTEMS
The vessel carries a variety of atmospheric control devices, including an Electrolytic Oxygen Generator, to enable the submarine to remain submerged for long periods of time without ventilating.

MACHINERY
Los Angeles is powered by a General Electric S6G nuclear reactor, which delivers pressurized hot water to the steam generator. This in turn drives the steam turbines.

Sonar

Sensors on the *Los Angeles* vessels include a BQR-15 passive-towed sonar array, stowed in a channel on the starboard side of the casing and streamed through a tube on the starboard diving plane.

Armament

Los Angeles-class submarines carry about 25 weapons launched by torpedo tubes, and all boats of the class are capable of launching Tomahawk cruise missiles in this way. The last 31 boats of this class also have 12 dedicated vertical launch (VLS) tubes for launching Tomahawks.

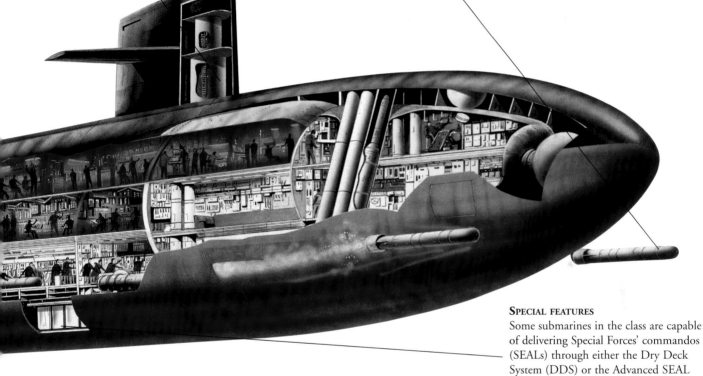

Special features

Some submarines in the class are capable of delivering Special Forces' commandos (SEALs) through either the Dry Deck System (DDS) or the Advanced SEAL Delivery System (ASDS).

LOS ANGELES (SSN 688) – SPECIFICATION

Country of origin: USA
Type: Submarine
Laid down: January 8, 1972
Builder: Newport News Shipbuilding
Launched: April 6, 1974
Commissioned: November 13, 1976
Decommissioned: January 23, 2010
Fate: Not available
Complement: 13 officers, 131 enlisted

Dimensions:
Displacement: 6,072 tons (5,508 tonnes)
Length: 361 ft 10 in (110.3 m);

Beam: 32 ft 10 in (10 m); **Draught:** 30 ft 10 in (9.4 m)

Power plant:
Propulsion: S6G nuclear reactor, 2 turbines, 1 shaft producing 35,000 shp (26 MW), 1 auxiliary motor producing 325 shp (242 kW)
Speed: (surfaced) 25 knots; (submerged) 30 knots
Range: Unlimited

Armament & Armor:
Armament: 4 x 21-in (533-mm) bow tubes, Mark 48 torpedo, Harpoon missile, Tomahawk cruise missile

The *Los Angeles*-class submarines were
intended mainly to escort carrier task groups.
For this reason, they were designed to be
capable of making high speeds underwater
in order to keep up with surface forces.

LOS ANGELES

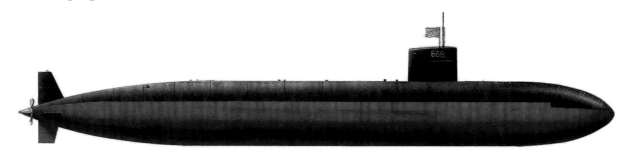

AMERICAN SSN: *SKIPJACK*

AMERICAN SSN: *PERMIT*

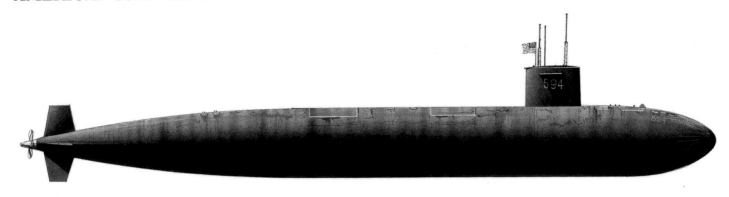

AMERICAN SSN: *STURGEON*

LOS ANGELES-CLASS TORPEDOES

The original primary weapon of the *Los Angeles*-class submarines was the 21-in (533-mm) heavyweight torpedo. A long-range, variable-speed, wire-guided dual-role weapon, it was developed beginning in 1957, when feasibility studies were initiated to meet an operational requirement that was eventually issued in 1960. The weapon was intended as both a surface- and submarine-launched torpedo, but the former requirement was dropped when surface-launched torpedoes were supplanted by anti-ship missiles. The latest variant is the Mk 48 MkMod 5, which has a higher-powered sonar to improve target acquisition and to reduce the effect of decoys and anechoic coatings.

This dramatic and atmospheric photograph shows a Los Angeles-*class submarine travelling at full speed on the surface, looking more like a colossal marine creature than a machine of war. In* Los Angeles, *the U.S. Navy acquired some of the fastest and quietest submarines ever built.*

The *Los Angeles* (SSN 688) was the lead ship in her class. She was launched in April 1974 and completed in November 1976. Total production was 62 units, making this class by far the most important in the U.S. submarine fleet.

Many important changes have been made to the "688s," as the class is commonly known, in the course of their operational life. Starting in 1984 onwards, beginning with the launch of the *Providence* (SSN 619), all the *Los Angeles*-class vessels have been fitted with vertical launch tubes for the Tomahawk land-attack cruise missile, 20 of which can be carried. Earlier vessels can launch Tomahawks from their torpedo tubes, but can only carry eight missiles.

STANDOFF LAND ATTACK

The launch of the *San Juan* (SSN 751) in 1986 marked the appearance of the "Improved 688" class because it was fitted with the new BSY-1 submarine combat system. A more obvious change was the replacement of the sail-mounted diving planes with bow planes, permitting better maneuverability when the boat was cruising under the ice.

Though they were designed as classic hunter-killer submarines, the role of the *Los Angeles* class has been greatly expanded in the modern U.S. Navy by virtue of a standoff land attack capability. In fact, the fleet of *Los Angeles* SSNs provides the U.S. with a second-tier attack force, quite distinct from the fleet ballistic missile submarines. U.S. Navy attack submarines have been capable of launching nuclear weapons, when the Regulus cruise missile was introduced on a limited scale. However, matching the *Los Angeles* class with the Tomahawk cruise missile has produced a truly deadly combination.

A VERSATILE ASSET

During the latter years of the Cold War, the *Los Angeles*-class SSNs would have gone to sea with some of their BGM-109 Tomahawk missiles armed with 200 KT thermonuclear warheads. The nuclear-tipped version of the Tomahawk is no longer deployed, and missiles now carry 1,000 lb (450 kg) of high explosive. This switch to the conventional land attack role has made her class a far more useful and versatile asset.

INVISIBLE PRESENCE

Submarines have a covert striking power and can be deployed to a crisis or potential trouble spot without ever betraying their presence. Nine of the class were involved in the Gulf War of 1991, two firing Tomahawk missiles at targets in Iraq from stations in the eastern Mediterranean,

and the *Los Angeles* boats have since supported NATO operations in the Balkans and Afghanistan.

Nineteen years after *Los Angeles* joined the fleet, the commissioning of *Cheyenne* (SSN-773) brought to a close the biggest group of SSNs ever built to a single design. The long production run was due to uncertainty about successors, and by the mid-1990s the design was starting to look dated.

Ten years later, *Los Angeles* was the oldest submarine still on active service with the U.S. Navy. She was inactivated on November 2, 2009, to await decommissioning and disposal at a later date.

Interior view

The sonar room on *Los Angeles* is where all the information from the boat's sensors is collated and interpreted. In effect, it is the eyes and ears of the submerged submarine.

(1) **Officer of the deck:** Supervised by the officer of the deck, each console is manned by a senior technician.

(2) **Consoles:** The sonar room is dominated by its consoles, each performing a specific function.

(3) **Lighting:** The color of the lighting can be altered to suit particular conditions; blue background lighting is often used.

(4) **Modes:** Two modes of sonar observation are used. In the "active" mode, the echoes of sound waves sent out from the sub are timed and analyzed by the operator.

(5) **Towed sonar:** This is the passive "thin line" array, designed to detect very low-frequency noise at very long ranges.

(6) **Intercept receiver:** An acoustic intercept receiver alerts the crew that an active sonar is being used.

Kirov/Admiral Ushakov 1977

When the Soviet Union launched the missile cruiser *Kirov* in December 1977, she was the largest warship – apart from aircraft carriers – built by any nation since World War II. She was reminiscent of the battlecruisers of bygone years.

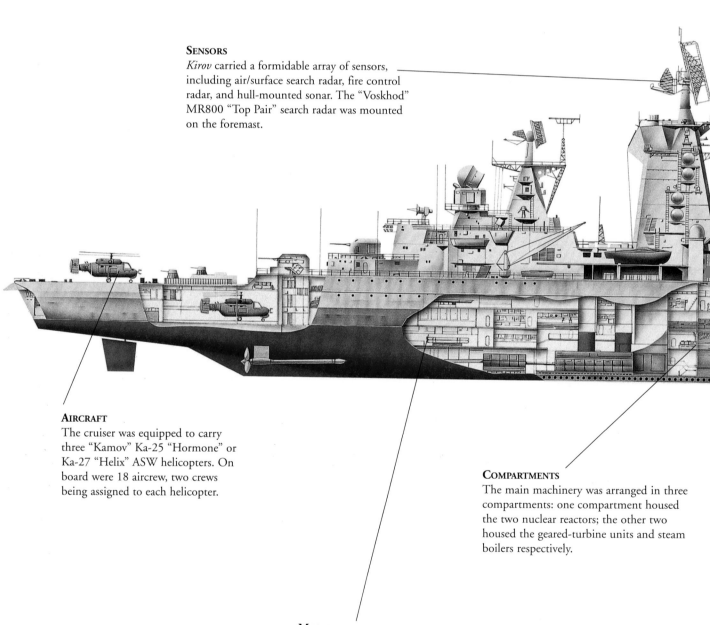

SENSORS
Kirov carried a formidable array of sensors, including air/surface search radar, fire control radar, and hull-mounted sonar. The "Voskhod" MR800 "Top Pair" search radar was mounted on the foremast.

AIRCRAFT
The cruiser was equipped to carry three "Kamov" Ka-25 "Hormone" or Ka-27 "Helix" ASW helicopters. On board were 18 aircrew, two crews being assigned to each helicopter.

COMPARTMENTS
The main machinery was arranged in three compartments: one compartment housed the two nuclear reactors; the other two housed the geared-turbine units and steam boilers respectively.

MACHINERY
Kirov's propulsion system was based on a combination of nuclear power and steam turbine, with two nuclear reactors coupled to two oil-fired boilers, which superheated the steam produced in the reactor plant to increase the power output available during high-speed running.

ARMAMENT
Primary armament of the *Kirov* was the "Granit" (SS-N-19 "Shipwreck") long-range anti-ship missile. Twenty missiles were installed under the upper deck, mounted at an angle of 60 degrees.

BOW
One of the prominent features of the *Kirov*-class warships was the sharply raked bow, a feature of all Soviet warships designed in the latter years of the Cold War.

F A C T S

- Launched December 26, 1977; commissioned December 30, 1980.

- First Soviet nuclear-powered surface warship.

- Assigned to the Soviet Northern Fleet.

- Reactor accident while on deployment to the Mediterranean, 1990.

- Placed in reserve and renamed *Admiral Ushakov*, 1992.

- Name *Admiral Ushakov* assigned to a destroyer, 2004.

- Awaiting dismantling in 2010.

KIROV/ADMIRAL USHAKOV – SPECIFICATION

Country of origin: Soviet Union
Type: Missile cruiser
Laid down: March 27, 1974
Builder: Baltiysky Naval Shipyard, Leningrad
Launched: December 26, 1977
Commissioned: December 30, 1980
Decommissioned: 1990
Fate: Awaiting dismantling
Complement: 727, aircrew 18, flagstaff 15

Dimensions:
Displacement: (full load) 28,000 tons (25,401 tonnes)
Length: 827 ft (252 m); **Beam:** 94 ft (28.5 m); **Draught:** 30 ft (9.1 m)

Power plant:
Propulsion: 2-shaft CONAS, nuclear-powered with steam turbine boost producing 140,000 shp (104.4 MW)
Speed: 32 knots
Range: 1,000 nm (1,852 km) at 30 knots; essentially unlimited with nuclear power at 20 knots

Armor & Armament:
Armament: 10 x 21-in (533-mm) torpedo tubes; 20 x SS-N-19 "Shipwreck" cruise missiles; 14 x SS-N-14 cruise missiles; rocket launchers, and guns
Armor: 3-in (76-mm) plating around reactor compartment
Aircraft: 3 x Kamov Ka-27 "Helix" or Ka-25 "Hormone" helicopters

Kirov was originally designed as a large anti-submarine warship to search for and engage enemy ballistic missile submarines. After the introduction of the Granit anti-ship missile system, its role was then expanded to engage large surface targets and to provide air and anti-submarine protection to naval forces.

KIROV

SOVIET CRUISER: *MOSKVA*

SOVIET CRUISER: "KARA"

SOVIET CRUISER: *KRASINA*

SOVIET SURPRISES

In the last three decades of the Cold War, Soviet naval architects produced many surprises. In December 1977, the Soviet navy – which by then had expanded its operations worldwide to become a true blue-water fleet – launched the nuclear-powered *Kirov*, the largest warship built by any nation since World War II apart from aircraft carriers. Designated *Raketnyy Kreyser*, the 24,000-ton (24,385-tonne) vessel was more akin, in terms of appearance and firepower, to the obsolete battlecruiser category. Three more vessels of the *Kirov* class were completed: the *Frunze*, *Kalinin*, and *Yuri Andropov*.

The Kirov *was one of the most handsome warships produced by Russian shipyards and was certainly one of the most effective. She has been photographed here at Severomorsk, the primary base of the Northern Fleet.*

In 1984, the Soviet Northern Fleet conducted a large-scale deployment to the Norwegian Sea. It was the largest exercise of its type yet seen. At its heart was the new nuclear-powered cruiser, *Kirov*.

The ability of the Russians to deploy so many warships and supporting units at one time – and with speed – alarmed NATO planners. If the Soviet navy could achieve similar surprise at the outset of a real conflict, it could secure the northern part of the Norwegian Sea and prevent deployment of NATO reinforcements to northern Norway in the event of a Soviet offensive. A further factor that alarmed the Supreme Allied Commander Atlantic (SACLANT) was not so much the current Soviet naval force levels, but the realization that the NATO nations were no longer numerically equal to their potential enemy in shipbuilding terms.

Another even more disquieting trend was the closing of the quality gap that SACLANT had once enjoyed over the

Warsaw Pact. This was due partly to the assimilation of huge amounts of published Western military technology that was freely available to the Warsaw Pact, but also to the enormous resources the Soviet Union had devoted to improving the capability of its naval forces. Each successive naval platform had far greater capability in terms of improved weapons and electronics, and an increased durability for sustained operations. By the mid-1980s, almost every unit in the Soviet maritime inventory was armed with a missile of some sort, including very effective sea-skimming anti-ship weapons.

THE "SHIPWRECK" MISSILE

In the case of *Kirov*, there was the Granit long-range anti-ship missile system, known in the West as the "Shipwreck" missile. Twenty Granit anti-ship missiles were installed under the upper deck, mounted at a 60-degree angle. The long-range missiles could not be controlled once launched, but they had what was known as a multivariant target engagement program. When ripple-fired, the missiles shared information while in flight. The lead missile assumed a high-level flight trajectory, enabling it to increase its target acquisition capability, while the other missiles followed at a lower level. If the lead missile was destroyed, one of the other missiles automatically assumed the lead role.

In 1990, the mighty *Kirov* suffered a reactor accident while deployed in the Mediterranean. Repairs were never carried out, partly because of a lack of funds and partly because of the rapidly changing political situation. As a result, in 1992, the warship was placed in reserve, laid up at Severomorsk and renamed *Admiral Ushakov* after an

eighteenth-century Russian naval officer. In 1999 Russia's lower parliament, the Duma, authorized repair work to be carried out on the warship, but it never happened. Instead, she was cannibalized for spare parts in order to keep her sister ships in commission.

Of the latter, *Frunze* was renamed *Admiral Lazarev* and by 2009 was awaiting deployment to the Pacific. *Kalinin* was mothballed in 1999 but was reactivated as *Admiral Nakhimov* in 2005, while *Yuri Andropov*, which was not commissioned until 1998, was renamed *Pyotr Velikiy* (Peter the Great) and by 2009 was serving as flagship of the Russian Northern Fleet.

Close-up

Kirov/Admiral Ushakov was fitted with state-of-the-art control and communications systems. Their sophistication came as something of a shock to Western naval analysts.

(1) Gunnery system: The main components of the gunnery system are a computer-based control system with a multi-band radar, television, and optical target sighting.

(2) Gun: The gun can be operated under fully automatic remote control interfaced to the radar control system.

(3) Modules: Two command modules and six combat modules are installed on the ship. The command module provides autonomous operation by detecting any threats.

(4) Target tracking: The combat module tracks the target with radar and television.

(5) Radar arrays: The main radar arrays are the Voskhod MR-800 (top pair) 3D search radar on the foremast, the Fregat MR-710 (top steer) 3D search radar on the main mast, and the "Palm Frond" navigation radar, on the foremast.

(6) Sonar: The cruiser is fitted with the "Horse Jaw" LF hull sonar and "Horse Tail" VDS (Variable Depth Sonar).

Seawolf (SSN-21) 1995

Seawolf-class submarines were designed to operate autonomously against the world's most capable submarine and surface threats. The primary mission of the *Seawolf* was to destroy Soviet ballistic missile submarines before they could attack American targets.

ELECTRONICS
Seawolf's electronics suite can integrate into a naval battle group's infrastructure, or shift rapidly into a land-battle support role.

PERISCOPES
Seawolf has two main periscopes, mounted in a sail that is specially strengthened for operations under the Arctic ice cap.

ARMAMENT
Seawolf has an eight-tube, double-deck torpedo room, enabling the boat to engage multiple threats. *Seawolf* has twice as many torpedo tubes and its weapons magazine is one-third larger in size than the earlier *Los Angeles*-class submarines.

SPECIAL OPERATIONS
The third *Seawolf*-class submarine, *Jimmy Carter*, is capable of supporting Special Operations Forces with provision for operating the Dry Deck Shelter (DDS) and Advanced SEAL Delivery System (ASDS). The DDS is an air-transportable device that piggybacks on the submarine and can be used to store and launch a swimmer delivery vehicle as well as combat swimmers.

MACHINERY

Seawolf is powered by one S6W reactor and is an extremely quiet boat with a very high tactical speed (the speed at which a submarine is still quiet enough to remain undetected while tracking enemy submarines effectively).

HULL

Construction of the *Seawolf*-class submarines relies on a new welding material to join the steel into plates, hull subsections, and large cylindrical sections. Their hulls are made entirely of high-pressure HY-100 steel. Previous submarine classes were made with HY-80 steel.

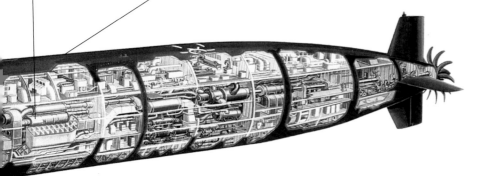

SEAWOLF – SPECIFICATION

Country of origin: USA
Type: Submarine
Laid down: October 25, 1989
Builder: General Dynamics Electric Boat, Connecticut
Launched: June 24, 1995
Commissioned: July 19, 1997. Still in service
Complement: 15 officers, 101 enlisted

Dimensions:
Displacement: (surfaced) 8,600 tons (7,802 tonnes); (submerged) 9,138 tons (8,290 tonnes)
Length: 353 ft (108 m); **Beam:** 40 ft (12 m);
Draught: 36 ft (11 m)

Power plant:
Propulsion: One S6W pressurized water-cooled reactor powering steam turbines delivering 45,000 hp (33.6 MW)
Speed: (submerged) 35 knots; (silent) 25 knots
Range: Unlimited

Armament & Armor:
Armament: 8 x 26-in (660-mm) torpedo tubes (with up to 50 Tomahawk cruise missiles; Mk 48 ADCAP torpedoes or 100 mines)
Armor: Unavailable

The approximate equivalent of *Seawolf* in the British Royal Navy is *Astute*, which was launched in 2007. She is armed with Tomahawk cruise missiles and, because her systems can purify both air and water, she can theoretically circumnavigate the globe without surfacing. In fact, her endurance is limited only by the amount of supplies she can carry.

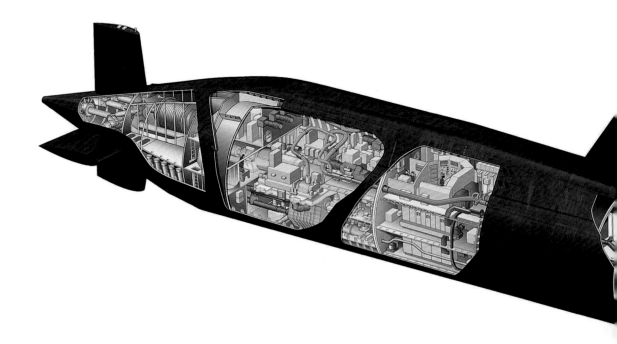

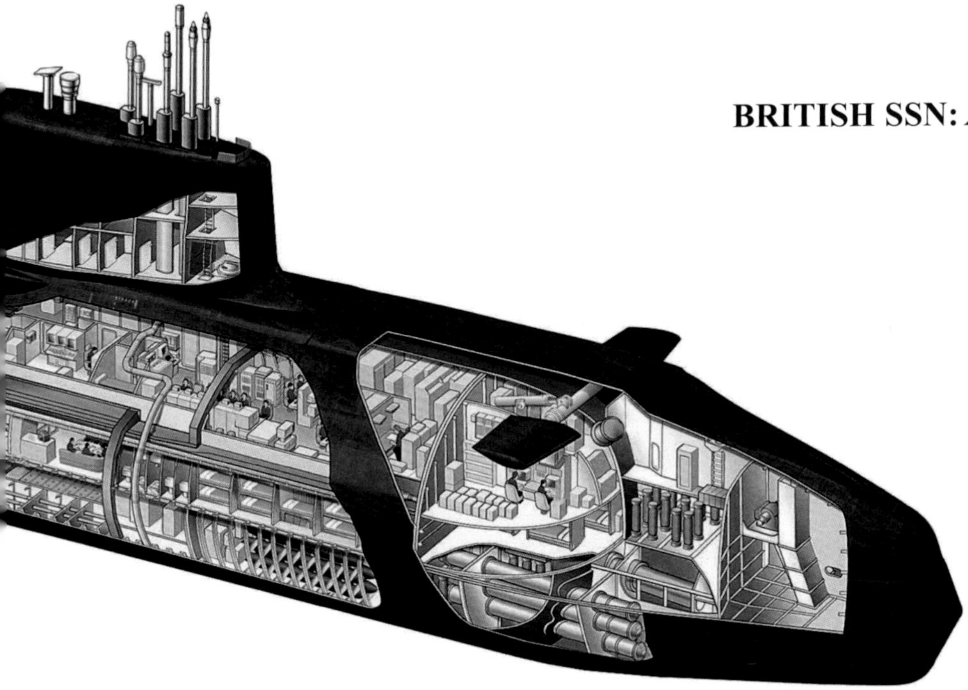

BRITISH SSN: *ASTUTE*

SEAWOLF CLASS

The *Seawolf* class was originally designed to counter the rapidly increasing capabilities of the Soviet submarine force projected for the 1990s and beyond. Quiet, fast, and well armed with advanced sensors, their primary purpose was to deploy to forward ocean areas to search out and destroy enemy submarines and surface ships, and to attack land targets. The robust design of the submarines enables them to perform a variety of crucial assignments from underneath the Arctic ice pack to littoral regions anywhere in the world. Their missions include surveillance, intelligence collection, special warfare, covert cruise-missile strikes, mine warfare, and anti-submarine and anti-surface ship warfare.

The Seawolf *(SSN-21) is photographed travelling at full speed on the surface. As indicated by the massive and turbulent wake, nuclear submarines are not meant for surface travel; their true environment is deep underwater.*

When Ronald Reagan became president in 1981, he was determined to reverse what most military people regarded as the decline in America's ability to defend itself against the Soviet Union.

The commanders of the U.S. Navy's submarine fleet advised the new president to go on the offensive. This meant penetrating the "bastions" of the USSR to engage Soviet submarines, rather than waiting behind defensive barriers until the Russians chose their moment to attack.

One result of this new policy was the development of *Seawolf*. The design that emerged had eight launch tubes, positioned just ahead of the forwards bulkhead of the pressure hull, and stowage for 50 torpedoes or anti-ship missiles. Its machinery was much quieter than that installed in the earlier *Los Angeles* class (with which U.S. submariners had expressed much dissatisfaction), and it

was more compact. The pumpjet propulsor would reduce cavitation (the formation of bubbles in the wake), reducing noise levels and still leaving the new SSN capable of 35 knots underwater. The new S6W reactor produced a power output of 50,000 hp (33.6 MW), while the electronics suite included the new BSY-2 command system, a spherical receiving sonar array, a linear transmitting array wrapped around the bow, the new TB-16E and TB-29 towed arrays, and other sensors.

FULLY INTEGRATED COMBAT SYSTEM

The BSY-2 is the U.S. Navy's first fully integrated submarine combat system, with all the sensors, data processors, consoles, and weapon controls riding the same high-capacity fiber-optic data bus. The consoles can be switched among the various command and control tasks, and the bus can handle 1,000 messages per second. The whole system is so complex that it requires nearly 157 gallons (600 liters) of chilled water per minute to cool it.

Seawolf is claimed to make less noise at a tactical speed of 25 knots than *Los Angeles* does when laid up beside a pier. Originally, 29 *Seawolf*s were planned for production, but with the end of the Cold War, the cost was judged to be prohibitively high and only three were built in favor of the smaller *Virginia* class, which are about 10 percent cheaper.

UNPRECEDENTED SPEED

Seawolf was launched on June 24, 1995, and began initial sea trials in July 1996. She demonstrated unprecedented speed during her first trial. Following delivery, *Seawolf* began acoustic trials, which were completed in November 1997. The second boat in the class, *Connecticut* (SSN-22) went to sea in 1998. The third and final *Seawolf*-class submarine, *Jimmy Carter* (SSN-23), was launched in 2004 and is outfitted with an additional hull section. This lengthens the ship for special missions and research and development projects. *Jimmy Carter* is roughly 98 ft (30 m) longer than the other two ships of her class. This is due to the insertion of a plug (additional section) known as the MMP (Multi-Mission Platform), which allows the launch and recovery of remotely controlled vehicles and special forces. *Jimmy Carter* also has additional maneuvering devices fitted fore and aft that allow it to keep station over selected targets in odd currents. In the past, submarines fitted with these devices were used to intercept communications by tapping into underwater cables.

Interior view

Nuclear submarines are generally fitted with two escape trunks, one situated forward and the other aft. Each trunk can accommodate two crew members at a time.

1. **Pressure vessel:** The escape trunk is composed of a pressure vessel about 8 ft (2.4 m) tall and 5 ft (1.5 m) in diameter, which is something of a tight squeeze.

2. **Immersion suits:** The crew are provided with immersion suits, bright red in color for ease of identification and location.

3. **Steinke hood:** Crew members use a "Steinke hood," a combination of life jacket and breathing apparatus that fits over the head.

4. **Hatch:** The top is a hatch capable of withstanding the same pressure as the hull of the boat.

5. **Air port:** There is an air port on the side of the trunk from which sailors charge their Steinke hoods prior to escape.

6. **Supplies:** In harbor, supplies and equipment are often loaded in the boat by way of the escape trunks.

Visby 2000

The *Visby*-class corvette is the latest class of corvette to be deployed with the Royal Swedish Navy after the *Göteborg* and *Stockholm* classes. The vessel has many stealth features, and the first two ships became operational early in 2010.

AIRCRAFT
Visby can carry one helicopter such as the AgustaWestland A109M. A helicopter hangar was originally planned, but was deleted because it was considered too cramped.

STRUCTURE
The hull is constructed with a sandwich design consisting of a PVC core with a carbon fiber and vinyl laminate. Its angular design reduces its radar signature.

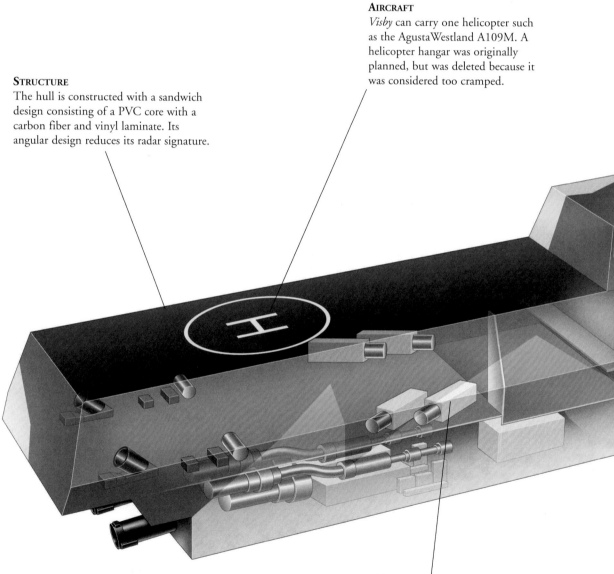

MACHINERY
Visby is powered by four Vericor TF50A turbines for high speed, plus two diesels for low speed with double flexible mountings, with encapsulated noise-absorbant housings.

- *Visby* is named after the principal city on the island of Gotland.

- The class was originally designed to be divided into two subcategories where some ships were optimized for surface combat and others for submarine hunting.

- *Visby* was launched in 2000.

- There are five ships in the class, the others being *Helsingborg*, *Härnösand*, *Nyköping*, and *Karlstad*.

- There was a delay of almost 10 years between the first ship being launched and the first two being delivered.

SYSTEMS

Visby carries hull-mounted, variable-depth and towed-array sonar systems. The vessel is fitted with a Condor CS-3701 Tactical Radar Surveillance System and a Ceros 200 fire control radar system.

ARMAMENT

Visby was designed to carry eight RBS15 anti-ship missiles, mines and depth charges, and vertical-launch surface-to-air missiles, but it was decided not to install the latter. A rapid-firing 2.24-in (57-mm) Bofors gun is mounted.

ROVs

The corvette is equipped with a compartment for housing and launching remotely controlled vehicles (ROVs) for hunting and destroying mines.

VISBY – SPECIFICATION

Country of origin: Sweden
Type: Corvette
Laid down: February 17, 1995
Builder: Kockums AB, Sweden
Launched: 2000
Commissioned: N/A
Complement: 27 officers, 16 conscripts

Dimensions:
Displacement: 650 tons (590 tonnes)
Length: 238 ft (72.6 m)
Beam: 34 ft (10.4 m)
Draught: 8.2 ft (2.5 m)

Power plant:
Propulsion: CODAG, 2 x Honeywell TF 50 A gas turbines, total rating 21,446 shp (16 MW), 2 x MTU Friedrichshafen 16V 2,000 N90 diesel engines, total rating 2,385 shp (2.6 MW)
Speed: 40 knots
Range: Not specified

Armament & Armor:
Armament: 1 x 2.24-in (57-mm) Mk3 gun; 8 x RBS15 Mk 2 anti-ship missile; plus mines and depth charges
Armor: N/A
Aircraft: Helicopter pad

The *Visby* class experienced exceptional delays between launch and delivery. By 2008, the only weapons system that had been integrated and tested on the *Visby* was the Bofors gun.

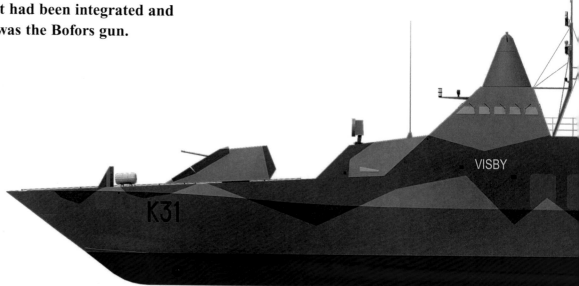

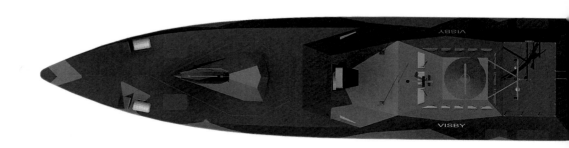

VISBY

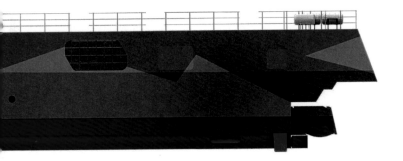

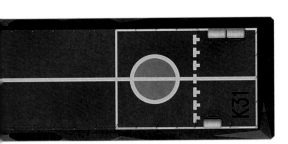

SWEDISH SURFACE WARSHIPS

Since the 1980s, Swedish surface warships have been named after Swedish cities, hence the nomenclature of *Visby* and her sister ships. Submarines are named after Swedish provinces, and minehunters after Swedish lighthouses. The surface ships are mostly small, a configuration dictated by the relatively shallow and confined waters of the Baltic Sea, relying on agility and flexibility to fulfill their tasks. In 1972 the Swedish government decided to scrap all military protection of merchant shipping to enable the decommissioning of destroyers and frigates. This limited the endurance of the navy considerably, but the use of smaller short-range ships was at the time deemed adequate by the government for anti-shipping missions along the coast and in the archipelago.

Looking very futuristic, the Helsingborg *(K32) is pictured slicing through the Baltic in a plume of spray. The barrel of the gun is folded back into the turret. The hull is constructed with a sandwich design consisting of a PVC core with a carbon fiber and vinyl laminate.*

Construction began in 1996 at Kockums' Kalrskrona yard. The *Visby* (K31) was launched in June 2000 and was delivered to the FMV (the Swedish Defense Materiel Administration) in June 2002 for fitting with weapons and combat systems.

From the outset, the design of the *Visby*-class corvettes placed heavy emphasis on stealth technology. *Visby* was the lead vessel and was launched in 2000. However, the entire progam was immediately beset by a succession of delays, caused not least by a reduction of funding caused by the apparent end of the Cold War. It was not until 2009 that *Visby* and a second vessel, *Helsingborg* (K32), were delivered to the Royal Swedish Navy. Even then, they lacked some of their planned weapon systems, resulting in a much reduced operational capability.

Much of the design of the *Visby* class was based on experience gained with an experimental ship, *Smyge*. The hull consists of a sandwich design comprising a PVC core with a carbon fiber and vinyl laminate, and its angular design greatly reduces the radar signature. Stealth

technology is also applied to other areas. For example, the barrel of the 2.24-in (57-mm) Bofors cannon can be folded into the turret to reduce its cross-section.

The *Visby* class was originally intended to be divided into two subcategories, one optimized for surface combat and the other for submarine hunting, but the roles were combined because of funding economies. The corvettes are equipped with a helicopter platform for operating general purpose/ASW helicopter such as the AgustaWestland A109M. A helicopter hangar was originally planned, but was deleted during the design phase because it was considered to be too cramped.

INTEGRATION AND TESTING

Fitting out and completion of the *Visby* corvettes has been slow. By 2008, eight years after launch, the only weapon system that had been integrated and tested on the *Visby* was the Bofors gun. The weapon has a fully automatic loading system containing 120 rounds of ready-to-fire ammunition and fires up to 220 rounds a minute to a maximum range of 10.5 miles (17,000 m). The integration and testing of the torpedo system remained incomplete when *Visby* was delivered in

2009, as was integration of the vessel's intended anti-ship missile, the RBS-15. The missile has a high subsonic speed, Mach 0.9, and is armed with a 441-lb (200-kg) warhead. The missiles will be installed belowdecks and fired through special hatches to maintain the vessel's stealth. The missiles' exhaust plumes will be dispersed in separate canals.

MINEHUNTING ROLE

The *Visby* class is equipped to carry Saab Bofors Underwater system ROVs (remotely operated vehicles) for mine hunting, and the Atlas Elektronik Seafox ROV for mine disposal. The minehunting ROVs are a development of the Double Eagle Mk III. The *Visby* corvettes are being fitted with the Hydra multi-sonar suite from General Dynamics Canada (formerly Computing Devices Canada), which integrates data from a Hydroscience Technologies passive towed array sonar, C-Tech CVDS-26 dual-frequency active variable depth sonar (VDS), C-Tech CHMS-90 hull-mounted sonar and data from the ROVs.

All systems were expected to be fully integrated in 2010–13, but full operational capability was not expected until 2013.

Interior view

A key feature of the *Visby*-class corvettes is their fully automated control center, designed to reduce the number of crew members and cut costs.

① **Command and control:** The vessel's CETRIS C³ (command, control, and communications) system consists of the Saab Systems 9LV Mk3E combat management system.

② **Open system:** The 9LV Mk3 is based on open system architecture and uses the Windows NT operating system.

③ **Communications:** The communications system has a high-capacity digital communications switch, developed by Danish company Maersk Data Defense.

④ **Radio links:** The system provides internal communications or open conference lines and access to external communications with various radio links.

⑤ **TRSS:** The CS-3701 tactical radar surveillance system (TRSS) provides electronic support measures (ESM) and radar warning receiver (RWR) functions.

⑥ **Integration:** The SaabTech CEROS 200 fire control system will be fully integrated into the combat management system.

Daring Type 45 2006

The Type 45 destroyer is a state-of-the-art air defense destroyer program, designed to replace the Type 42 destroyers in service with the British Royal Navy. The Type 45s are also known as the *Daring* class after the lead ship of the same name.

STEALTH FEATURES
The Type 45 incorporates signature reduction features, including the elimination of right angles and reduced equipment on deck. The infrared signature is reduced by cooling devices on the funnels.

AIR DEFENSE
The Type 45 design uses the Principal Anti-Air Missile System (PAAMS), a joint British, French, and Italian design. The PAAMS system is able to control and coordinate several missiles in the air at once.

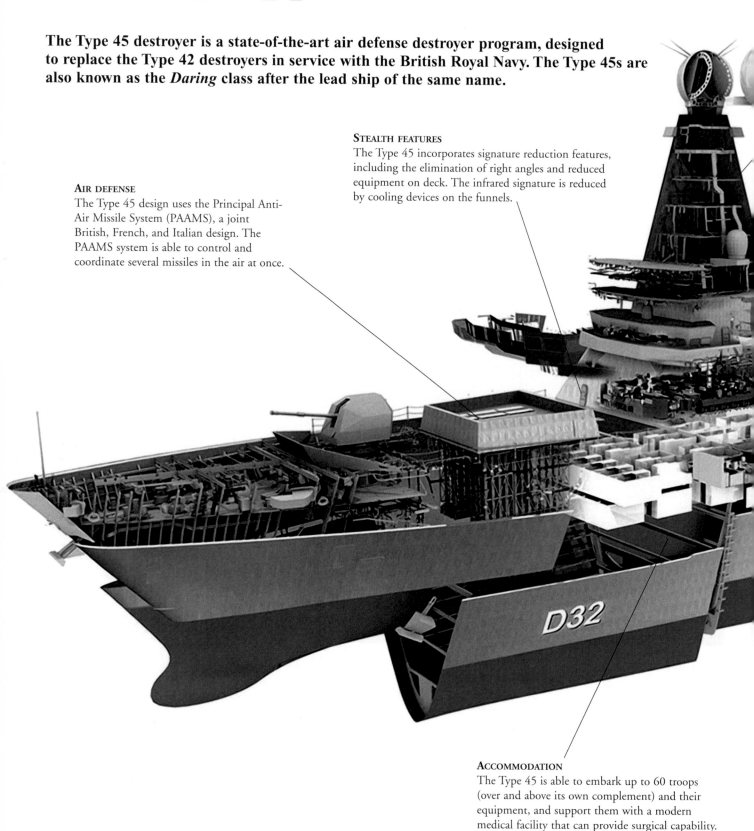

ACCOMMODATION
The Type 45 is able to embark up to 60 troops (over and above its own complement) and their equipment, and support them with a modern medical facility that can provide surgical capability.

RADAR

Daring's SAMPSON radar is said to be capable of tracking an object the size of a tennis ball traveling at three times the speed of sound.

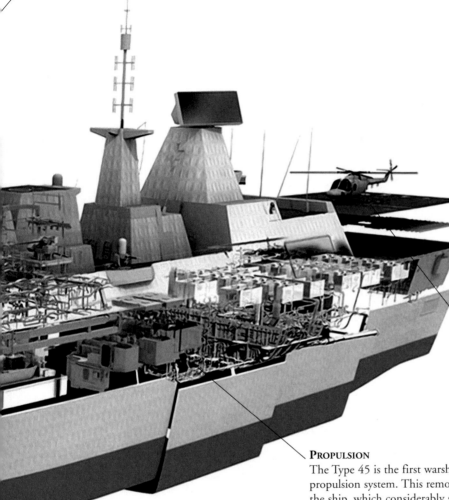

FLIGHT DECK

The Type 45 has a large flight deck that can accommodate helicopters up to and including the size of a Chinook. The ship can also take up to 700 people if necessary to support a civilian evacuation from war zones or natural disasters.

PROPULSION

The Type 45 is the first warship to use an all-electric propulsion system. This removes the need for a gearbox on the ship, which considerably simplifies maintenance and also reduces the amount of layup time.

DARING TYPE 45 – SPECIFICATION

Country of origin: United Kingdom
Type: Guided missile destroyer
Laid down: March 28, 2003
Builder: BAE Systems Surface Ships
Launched: February 1, 2006
Commissioned: July 23, 2009
Complement: 190

Dimensions:
Displacement: (deep load) 9,000 tons (8,092 tonnes)
Length: 500 ft (152.4 m)
Beam: 69.5 ft (21.2 m)
Draught: 16.4 ft (7.4 m)

Power plant:
Propulsion: 2 x Rolls-Royce WR-21 gas turbines producing 28,819 shp (21.5 MW), 2 Converteam electric motors producing 26,808 shp (20 MW)
Speed: 29 knots
Range: 7,000 nm (12,964 km) at economical speed

Armament & Armor:
Armament: 1 x PAAMS Air Defense System SYLVER CLS of Aster 15 and Aster 30 missiles; 2 x Phalanx CIWS; 1 x BAE 4.5-in (115-mm) Mk 8 mod 1 gun; 2 x 1.18-in (30-mm) guns
Armor: N/A
Aircraft: 1 x Lynx HMA8 or 1 x Westland Merlin HM1 helicopter

The Type 45 may be fitted with cruise missiles in the future, should the need arise. The most likely candidate is a naval version of the Storm Shadow missile, already operated by the RAF.

EVOLUTION OF THE DESTROYER

Since World War II, the destroyer has evolved from a torpedo-armed, all-gun surface warfare vessel into a specialist anti-air or anti-submarine ship, capable of either independent operations for a short time or of operating as an escort in a task force. The losses suffered by the Royal Navy's destroyers during the Falklands War proved to NATO that the UK's minimally armed warships, which had been constructed to satisfy constraints imposed by the UK Treasury, were extremely vulnerable in a conventional war, let alone the nuclear scenarios that were then proposed for any future conflict in the North Atlantic theater of operations. Any new design would have to be completely fit for purpose, as the Type 45s are.

TYPE 45

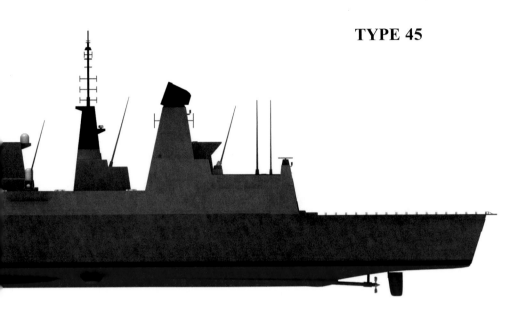

The *Daring* class destroyers are significantly larger than the Type 42s that they replaced, displacing about 8,101 tons (7,350 tonnes) compared to 5,732 tons (5,200 tonnes) of the Type 42. Their range is also about one-third greater, thanks to their advanced propulsion system.

Launched on February 1, 2006, *Daring* (D32) successfully completed her stage-one sea trials in 2007. Of the other ships in the class, *Dauntless, Diamond, Dragon,* and *Defender* were respectively launched between 2007 and 2009, with the sixth, *Duncan,* expected to follow in October 2010. The Type 45 destroyers will provide the backbone of the Royal Navy's air defenses for the first half of the twenty-first century, and will be able to engage targets simultaneously and defend aircraft carriers or groups of ships against the strongest future threats from the air.

Close-up

Daring is seen here under construction at BAE Systems, Scotstoun, on the Clyde River. She is claimed to be the most advanced air defense warship in the world.

(1) **Gantry:** The warship is surrounded by a large gantry, or cradle, that is a prominent feature of every ship construction yard.

(2) **Main armament:** *Daring*'s main gun armament of one 4.5-in (114-mm) gun is being lowered into position at the forward end of the ship.

(3) **Secondary armament:** *Daring*'s gun armament also comprises two 1.18-in (30-mm) weapons, mounted on either side amidships.

(4) **Radar:** The Type 45's SAMPSON radar system is slowly taking shape. The structure will eventually be fully enclosed.

(5) **Stealth:** Even at this stage in her construction, *Daring*'s angular stealth features are clearly visible.

(6) **Missile launch:** Just behind the forward gun turret mounting, not visible here, is the vertical launch system for the ship's short- and long-range missiles.

Despite their angular appearance, the Daring-*class Type 45s are handsome vessels. Throughout the years, seven classes of warship have carried the name* Daring.

A versatile design, the Type 45 will provide unprecedented detection and defense and will contribute to worldwide maritime and joint operations in multi-threat environments, providing a specialist air-warfare capability.

Daring's main armament is the Principal Anti-Air Missile System, a surface-to-air missile system developed under a tri-national program by France, Italy, and the UK. This advanced weapons system will defend the Type 45, her consorts, and other task force vessels against highly maneuverable hostile incoming aircraft approaching at subsonic and supersonic speed, individually or in salvoes. The Type 45 could also accommodate cruise missiles and anti-ballistic missile systems should this requirement be identified in the future. The Type 45 will be able to operate a helicopter up to the size of a Chinook or Merlin, but will initially operate with Westland Lynx HMA.8 helicopters armed with Stingray torpedoes.

ALL-ELECTRIC PROPULSION SYSTEM

The Type 45 is the first warship to use an all-electric propulsion system. This removes the need for a gearbox on the ship, which considerably simplifies maintenance and should thus reduce the amount of layup time the ships experience. It also means that either of the turbines can be used to run the ship alone at a lower speed; higher speeds are achievable by simply starting up the other turbines. Combined with the use of highly efficient WR21 gas turbines, this is expected to make the Type 45s highly fuel-efficient, reducing their life cycle costs. As a result of this engine efficiency, the Type 45 has a range of some 7,000 nm (12,964 km), as compared to the Type 42's 4,000 nm (7,408 km). During sea trials in August 2007, *Daring* reached her design speed of 29 knots in 70 seconds and achieved a speed of 31.5 knots in 120 seconds.

DESIGNED FOR STEALTH

Operationally, one of the Type 45's outstanding attributes is stealth. The design of the Type 45 brings unprecedentedly low levels of radar signature to the Royal Navy. Deck equipment has been reduced to produce a very clean superstructure similar to that of the French *La Fayette* class of frigates. Berthing equipment and life rafts are concealed behind superstructure panels and, externally, the mast is very sparingly equipped, reducing the clutter that increases the radar signature.

Glossary

AA Anti-aircraft, as in anti-aircraft artillery (AAA); air-to-air, as in air-to-air missile (AAM).

Ahead-Astern Forward; backward (in reverse).

ASW Anti-submarine warfare.

Axial fire Gunfire ahead or astern, along the major axis of the vessel.

Ballast The weight added to a ship or boat to bring her to the desired level of floatation and to increase stability. Originally in the form of gravel, later metal and sometimes concrete, now more commonly water, which has the advantage of being easy to remove and replace.

Barbette Originally an open-topped armored enclosure, inside of which a gun was mounted on a turntable. The addition of an armored hood, which rotated with the gun mount, turned it into a turret. Later, the fixed (armored) cylinder upon which a turret rotated.

Battlecruiser The made-up designation for a hybrid warship armed like a battleship but sacrificing passive protection in the form of armor plate for speed.

Battleship Originally the biggest and most powerful ships of the fleet, mounting guns of usually 10 in (254 mm) or larger caliber (the biggest were those of the Japanese Yamato class, which were 18.1 in (460 mm), and heavily armored.

Beam The width of a ship's hull.

Bofors A Swedish armaments manufacturer, best known for its 1.6 in (40 mm) anti-aircraft gun. First produced in the 1930s and adopted widely from 1942, the recoil-actuated 40mm L/60 Bofors was the most effective weapon of its type; improved versions were still in production at the end of the 20th century.

Boom A spar used to extend the foot of a sail; also a floating barrier, usually across the entrance to a harbor.

Breech block The removable part of a gun's breech, through which projectile and charge could be loaded.

Caliber The diameter of the bore of a gun barrel; the number of times that diameter fits into the length of the barrel, expressed as "L/(caliber)"; e.g., a gun of 10 in bore with a barrel 300 in long would be described as "10 in L/30", or just "10 in/30."

Clipper An ultimately meaningless term used to describe any fast sailing ship, particularly one engaged in the grain, opium or tea trades, widely used in the mid-19th century.

Cruiser A warship, larger than a frigate or destroyer, much more heavily armed and often armored to some degree, intended for independent action or to act as a scout for the battlefleet.

Displacement A measure of the actual total weight of a vessel and all she contains obtained by calculating the volume of water she displaces.

Draught (also Draft) The measure of the depth of water required to float a ship, or how much she "draws."

Dreadnought The generic name given to a battleship modelled after HMS *Dreadnought*, the first with all-big-gun armament; it fell into disuse once all capital ships were of this form.

Forecastle Originally the superstructure erected at the bows of a ship to serve as a fighting platform, later the (raised) forward portion and the space beneath it, customarily used as crews' living quarters. Pronounced fo'c'sle.

Frigate Originally, fifth- or sixth-rate ships carrying their guns on a single deck, employed as scouts, and the counterpart of the later cruiser.

Gundeck The name given to the main deck in sailing warships of the British Royal Navy.

Ironclad The contemporary name for wooden warships clad with iron, and by extension, to the first iron warships; it continued in use up until the arrival of the dreadnought.

Jib A triangular sail (usually loose-footed) set on a forestay.

Knot Internationally, the measure of a ship's speed – one nautical mile per hour.

Lee/Leeward The side of the vessel away from the wind, but a coast onto which the wind is blowing.

Liner A ship carrying passengers to a fixed schedule, usually on trans-oceanic routes; the term became current from the mid-1800s. A cargo liner also operates on fixed schedules, with space for a limited number of passengers.

Magazine Secure storage for explosives.

Nautical mile Internationally, the measure of distance at sea that has become standardized at 6,080 ft (1,852 m).

Poop The short raised deck at the stern of a vessel, originally known as the aftercastle. The word is derived from the Latin *puppis*, stern.

Quarterdeck That part of the upper deck abaft the mainmast (or where the mainmast would logically be in a steam- or motor ship), traditionally the reserve of commissioned officers.

Radar An acronym for Radio Direction and Range – a means of using electromagnetic radiation to locate an object in space by bouncing signals off it and measuring the time elapsed before they return to the plane of the emitter, the orientation of the receiving antenna provides directional data.

Ram A strengthened, usually armored, projection from the bow of a warship, designed to allow her to pierce the hull of an adversary with relative impunity. Widely used in the age of the galley, it fell into disuse with the coming of sail, but enjoyed a brief revival after the Battle of Lissa in 1866, and was found on most major warships from just after that date until the coming of the dreadnoughts, even though it actually figured in more peacetime disasters than ever it did in wartime successes.

Reefer A refrigerated cargo-carrier.

Reserve Warships not in active commission are said to be in reserve; this may be a temporary measure, in which case maintenance work will be kept fully up to date, or a long-term measure, in which case the ship will be "mothballed" – effectively sealed up, with precautions taken to ensure that any machinery liable to deteriorate is well protected.

Rifle/Rifling The practice of cutting a series of grooves in a spiral the length of a gun's barrel, in order to impart spin to a projectile and thus stabilize it in flight. The system was widely adopted for naval ordnance from the mid-1800s; see also *smooth-bore*.

SAM Surface-to-air missile.

sc single class.

Schnorkel/Snorkel A tube with a ball-valve at its upper extremity, which allows a submarine to take in air, and thus continue to operate its internal-combustion engines, while remaining below the surface. Invented in the Netherlands in the 1930s, it was not used extensively until the German Navy took it up during World War II, but since then it has been universal.

Sheer The upward curve of a ship's upper deck towards bow and stern.

Smooth-bore A gun with a smooth (i.e., unrifled) barrel, used as naval ordnance until the second half of the 19th century.

Sonar An acronym for Sound Navigation and Ranging, a technique of using sound waves to detect objects underwater, and by extension, to the hardware employed.

Sponson A platform built outside the hull, at main or upper-deck level, usually to allow guns on the broadside to be sited so as to allow them to fire axially.

Squadron In the British Royal Navy, originally an organized unit of (usually eight) major warships – cruisers and capital ships, but in the U.S. Navy (and the practice became widespread), an organized unit of ships of any type, from minesweepers upwards, the term having taken over from flotilla.

Square-rigged A sailing vessel whose sails are set on yards, which when at rest are at right angles to the longitudinal axis of the hull.

SSM Surface-to-surface missile.

SSN Nuclear-powered submarine.

Standing rigging That portion of a ship's rigging—stays and shrouds, for example—that is employed to steady her masts.

Steam turbine A rotary engine in which steam is used to drive turbine blades arranged upon a shaft; invented by Parsons at the end of the 19th century.

Stem The foremost member of a ship's frame, fixed at its lower extremity to the keel.

Stern post The aftermost member of a ship's frame, fixed at its lower extremity to the keel.

Strake A structural timber running the length of a ship or boat's hull, along the major axis.

Submarine Properly speaking, a vessel capable of indefinite (or at least very prolonged) underwater operation; early submarines were in fact submersibles, and it was not until the advent of air-independent propulsion systems that true submarines were constructed.

Tack The lower forward corner of a fore-and-aft sail; a reach sailed (in a sailing vessel) with the wind kept on one side.

Tiller A wooden or metal bar attached rigidly to the rudder and used to control its movement.

Tonnage The load-carrying capacity of a merchant ship or the displacement of a warship.

Topmast The second section of a mast, stepped above the lower mast, carrying the (upper and lower) topmast yard(s).

Topping lift A rope or wire tackle by means of which a spar is lifted.

Transom A squared-off stern form, adopted both because it saved weight and resulted in better hydrodynamic performance.

Turret Originally an armored shell or covering for a gun, which rotated with the platform upon which the gun is mounted; later the armored cover became an integral part of the rotating mounting, and itself supported the gun or guns.

VLCC/ULCC Very/Ultra-Large Crude Carrier; the biggest oil tankers, with a deadweight capacity of over 200,000 tons (VLCC) and over 300,000 tons (ULCC).

For More Information

American Society of Naval Engineers (ASNE)
1452 Duke Street
Alexandria, VA 22314
(703) 836-6727
Web site: http://www.navalengineers.org
ASNE is a society for professionals who conceive, design, develop, test, construct, outfit, operate, and maintain naval and maritime ships, submarines, and aircraft. ASNE advances the knowledge and practice of naval engineering and promotes this career field.

Historic Naval Ships Association (HNSA)
P.O. Box 401
Smithfield, VA 23431-0401
(757) 356-9422
Web site: http://www.hnsa.org
This organization supports the preservation of historic naval vessels, educates the public, and honors the men and women who defend their nations at sea.

Intrepid Sea, Air & Space Museum
Pier 86, West 46th Street and 12th Avenue
New York, NY 10036-4103
(877) 957-SHIP [7447]
Web site: http://www.intrepidmuseum.org
This museum is housed in the aircraft carrier USS *Intrepid*, which served in World War II and Vietnam. The *Intrepid* was also used for submarine surveillance during the Cold War and as a recovery vessel for NASA. Artifacts, video footage, and interactive exhibits chronicle the history of the aircraft carrier and her crew.

Maritime Command Museum
Admiralty House
P.O. Box 99000, Station Forces
Halifax, NS B3K 5X5
Canada
(902) 721-8250
Web site: http://psphalifax.ca/marcommuseum
This museum was established to preserve the military heritage of Canada's Maritime Forces. The collection consists of an extensive research library, uniforms, model ships, medals, badges, shipboard memorabilia, armaments, and other artifacts of naval life.

National Museum of the U.S. Navy
805 Kidder Breese Street SE
Washington Navy Yard, DC 20374-5060
(202) 433-4882
Web site: www.history.navy.mil/nmusn
This museum chronicles the history of the U.S. Navy from its creation to the present. Featured artifacts include the USS *Constitution's* fighting top, the world's deepest diving submersible, *Trieste*, and the uniform of former Fleet Admiral Chester W. Nimitz.

Submarine Force Library and Museum
Home of the Historic Ship Nautilus
1 Crystal Lake Road
Groton, CT 06349-5571
(800) 343-0079
Web site: http://www.ussnautilus.org
The U.S. Navy operates this submarine museum, which houses thousands of artifacts, documents, and photographs relating to U.S. Submarine Force history. It is also home to the USS *Nautilus*, the first nuclear-powered ship and the first submarine to pass under the Arctic ice cap.

Vancouver Maritime Museum
1905 Ogden Avenue in Vanier Park
Vancouver, BC V6J 1A3
Canada
(604) 257-8300
Web site: http://www.vancouvermaritimemuseum.com
This museum preserves and educates the public about Canada's maritime history, art, culture, industry, and technology.

Web Sites

Due to the changing nature of Internet links, Rosen Publishing has developed an online list of Web sites related to the subject of this book. This site is updated regularly. Please use this link to access the list:

http://www.rosenlinks.com/wow/ships

For Further Reading

Adams, Simon. *Warships* (War Machines). Mankato, MN: Smart Apple Media in association with Imperial War Museum, 2009.

Ballard, Robert D., and Rick Archbold. *Robert Ballard's Bismarck*. Edison, NJ: Chartwell Books, 2007.

Bonner, Kit, and Carolyn Bonner. *Modern Warships* (Gallery). St. Paul, MN: Zenith Press, 2007.

Christley, Jim. *U.S. Nuclear Submarines: The Fast Attack* (New Vanguard). New York, NY: Osprey Publishing, 2007.

Dougherty, Martin J. *Sea Warfare*. New York, NY: Gareth Stevens Publishing, 2010.

Friedman, Norman. *Naval Firepower: Battleship Guns and Gunnery in the Dreadnought Era*. Annapolis, MD: Naval Institute Press, 2008.

Grant, R. G. *Battle at Sea*. New York, NY: DK Publishing, 2008.

Hore, Peter, and Bernard Ireland. *The World Encyclopedia of Battleships and Cruisers: A Complete Illustrated History of International Naval Warships from 1860 to the Present Day Shown in Over 1,200 Archive Photographs*. London, England: Lorenz, 2010.

Ireland, Bernard. *The History of Aircraft Carriers: An Authoritative Guide to 100 Years of Aircraft Carrier Development, from the First Flights from Ships in the Early 1900s Through to the Present Day*. London, England: Southwater, 2008.

Jackson, Robert. *101 Great Warships* (101 Greatest Weapons of All Times). New York, NY: Rosen Publishing, 2010.

Litwiller, Roger. *Warships of the Bay of Quinte*. Toronto, Canada: Dundurn Press, 2011.

McBride, William M. *Technological Change and the United States Navy, 1865–1945*. Baltimore, MD: Johns Hopkins University Press, 2010.

O'Hara, Vincent P., W. David Dickson, and Richard Worth. *On Seas Contested: The Seven Great Navies of the Second World War*. Annapolis, MD: Naval Institute Press, 2010.

Silverstone, Paul H. *The Navy of the Nuclear Age, 1947–2007* (U.S. Navy Warship). New York, NY: Routledge, 2009.

Index

About the Author

Robert Jackson is a writer on naval, aviation, and military affairs. He has more than ninety books to his name, including *The Encyclopedia of Ships* and *The Royal Navy in World War II*.